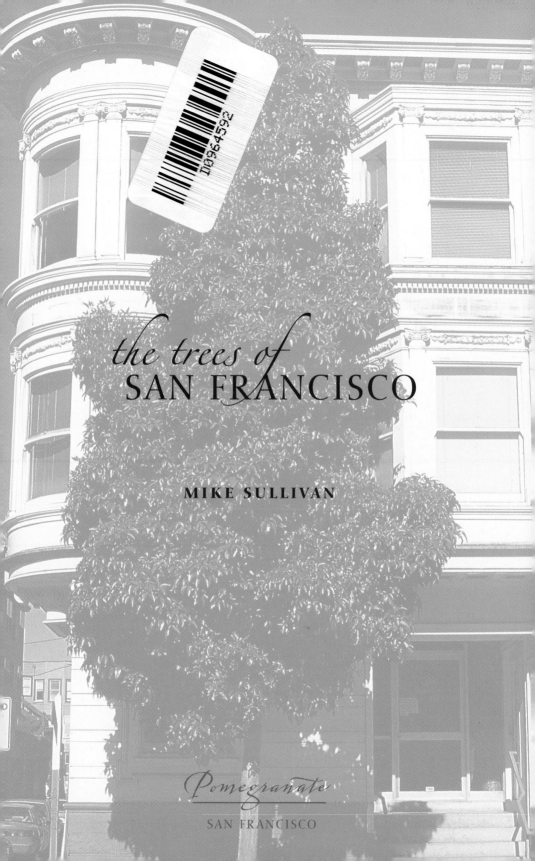

the trees of
SAN FRANCISCO

MIKE SULLIVAN

Pomegranate

SAN FRANCISCO

Published by Pomegranate Communications, Inc.
Box 808022, Petaluma CA 94975
800 227 1428; www.pomegranate.com

Pomegranate Europe Ltd.
Unit 1, Heathcote Business Centre
Hurlbutt Road, Warwick
Warwickshire CV 34 6TD, U.K.
44 1926 43011

Library of Congress Cataloging–in–Publication Data
Sullivan, Michael J., 1959–
    The trees of San Francisco / Michael J. Sullivan.
      p. cm.
    Includes bibliographical references (p. 147) and indexes.
      ISBN 0-7649-2758-2 (alk. paper)
      1. Trees–California–San Francisco–Identification. 2. Trees–California–San
Francisco–Pictorial works. 3. Trees–California–San Francisco–Guidebooks. 4. San
Francisco (Calif.)–Guidebooks. I. Title.

QK149.S85 2004
582.16'09794'61–dc22   2003062204

Pomegranate Catalog No. A709

Photographers
Jaime Pandolfo pp. 12 (top), 15, 17, 18, 26–29 30 (top), 34, 35, 39, 41, 43, 45, 46 (top),
47, 48, 50, 52 (bottom), 54, 55, 60, 61, 65 (top), 67, 69, 72, 73, 75, 77, 82, 83, 86, 88 (top), 89, 90,
94, 99, 145; *Mike Sullivan* 12 (bottom), 13, 14, 16, 19–22, 24, 25, 30 (bottom), 31, 33, 36, 38, 40,
42, 44, 49, 52 (top), 53, 55, 57–59, 62, 63, 66, 68, 70, 71, 76, 80, 81, 87, 88 (bottom), 91, 93,
95–98; *Friends of the Urban Forest* 11; *Paul Loeffler* 23; *Mark Bittner* 32; © *Chloe Atkins* 46, 65;
Remy Krzyzanowski 92

Tour maps and map of San Francisco: Lisa Reid

Design by India Ink, Petaluma, California

Printed in Korea

13 12 11 10 09 08 07 06 05 04   10 9 8 7 6 5 4 3 2 1

The true meaning of life is to plant trees, under whose shade you do not expect to sit.

—Nelson Henderson

To Joseph, who I hope will enjoy the shade of many of these trees.

CONTENTS

Sidelights

Tour Maps

PREFACE

Writing this book allowed me to combine two passions: trees and San Francisco.

I've always had a love for trees. I grew up in the hardwood forests of upstate New York, with maples, beeches, birches, and oaks; palm trees were things you saw on television in exotic vacation locales (like California). So when I moved to San Francisco in 1984, I was surprised to discover an entire urban forest that was almost completely alien to me—full of trees with strange shapes, exotic scents, unusual bark, colorful flowers, and leaves that stayed on the trees year-round. The one unifying feature was their unfamiliarity.

A few years later, I began volunteering with San Francisco's nonprofit tree group, Friends of the Urban Forest. Over many years of Saturday morning plantings and tree-care days with this organization, I became acquainted with the exotic trees from around the world that find their way to San Francisco's streets. As I got to know the trees of San Francisco, I became familiar with their stories—their origins, histories, smells, textures and shapes, reproductive tricks, and relationships with *Homo sapiens.*

I knew the moment I saw San Francisco in 1983 that I would live there. Like many before me, my immediate attachment to San Francisco was partly a reaction to the sheer physical beauty of the place. But over time, the real attraction became the neighborhoods—unique, bohemian, beautiful, vibrant neighborhoods, each with a distinctive personality, and each eminently walkable. I have enjoyed countless hours walking the streets of San Francisco, sometimes with purpose, more often with none, or at least with no purpose other than the joy of discovery. I found that my growing appreciation of the city's trees helped me to enjoy my walks—and San Francisco—even more. Each block had the potential for something new, and just as some people delight in coming upon a stunning Victorian home, a thriving *Ginkgo biloba* did the same for me.

I hope this book brings the same joy to those who read it—both to those of you who live here and to those of you who are visiting. For the San Francisco resident, here is an opportunity to learn about the trees you have walked past every day, trees that form the living part of the outdoor architecture in which we live. For the tourist (especially if you're from the land of maples and beeches, like me), this book is a chance to experience the new and the exotic.

I wrote this book primarily for the nonexpert, as a brief introduction to the trees of San Francisco. I am a botany amateur myself, so it has not been difficult to soft-pedal botanical vocabulary and details, except where I thought they would interest the average reader. That is the real goal of this book: to pique the interest of the average reader in the fascinating trees encountered on the streets of San Francisco every day.

Unlike other books of this type, this one is not an exhaustive list of all the different trees in San Francisco, nor a list of the largest or most impressive of the city's trees. Instead, this book details San Francisco's most common trees—so odds are good that the tree in front of your home is covered—and highlights a selection of less-common trees that I think are particularly interesting for one reason or another.

This book identifies hundreds of landmark trees in San Francisco, directing the reader to addresses where specific trees can be found. However, urban trees have a tendency to disappear—they get hit by trucks or cars, succumb to disease, or sometimes get removed by owners who want to improve their view. Fortunately, my website at www.sftrees.com supplies updates; just click on the Book Update section to find new information. I also have an e-mail link on the website, in case you have information to share, or you want to contact me for any other reason.

I would like to thank the many people who helped me write this book. Linda Liebelt of San Francisco's Academy of Sciences piqued my interest in local trees by introducing me to the botanical surprises to be found in San Francisco's urban forest. Arthur Lee Jacobson, author of *Trees of Seattle,* first planted in my head the idea of writing this book, and he and Scot Medbury, executive director of Strybing Arboretum in Golden Gate Park, have been generous with their time in reviewing the manuscript and correcting errors. Publishing attorney and friend Gray Coleman introduced me to Pomegranate, and was always there with advice for a first-time author. Doug Wildman, Ellyn Shea, Chris Buck, Alexis Harte, and others from Friends of the Urban Forest have been helpful over the years in introducing me to the trees of San Francisco and making available that organization's data on the city's trees. Photographer Jaime Pandolfo spent many hours hunting down trees in the four corners of San Francisco, and his skill and artistry made this book possible. Chloe Atkins and Remy Krzyzanowski also contributed beautiful photographs. Mark Bittner, Hank Donat, Rigo 04, the family of Victor Reiter, Emma Seager, and Barbara Stevens all contributed helpful information and content to these pages. Finally, I want to thank my tree-tortured but ultimately tree-tolerant partner, Paul Loeffler, for his patience in putting up with the many hours that went into the research and writing of this book.

introduction

Trees can have a hard time in San Francisco. Before the arrival of Europeans in the Bay Area, San Francisco was largely treeless, its grassy hills interrupted by only a few live oaks and California buckeyes huddled in wind-sheltered valleys. Shortly after arriving in San Francisco in 1776, the Spanish described the area as "the very worst place [for settlement] in all California . . . since the peninsula afforded neither lands, timber, wood, nor water, nothing but sand, brambles, and raging winds." To understand what San Francisco looked like in its natural state 200 years ago, just gaze across the Golden Gate to the Marin headlands, where you'll see grassy, windswept hills—and no trees.

Despite 150 years of recent human settlement, San Francisco's urban forest is a relatively recent phenomenon. Early tree-planting efforts focused almost exclusively on public parks. Beginning in 1870, the creation of Golden Gate Park out of acres of sand dunes was the most ambitious of these efforts. Landscape architect Frederick Law Olmsted, designer of New York's Central Park, submitted an early design for a great city park in 1865. His design was not accepted, and Olmsted later warned: "There is not a full grown tree of beautiful proportions near San Francisco, nor have I seen any young trees that promised fairly, except, perhaps, of certain compact clump forms of evergreens, wholly wanting in grace and cheerfulness. It would not be wise nor safe to undertake to form a park upon any plan which assumed as a certainty that trees which would delight the eye can be made to grow near San Francisco." In spite of Olmsted's warnings, the city persevered. The design job went to 24-year-old William Hammond Hall (later the park's first superintendent), and Golden Gate Park became the celebrated heart of San Francisco's urban forest.

Despite early successes in creating tree-filled parks, San Francisco's streets were bare for many more years. Look at any photograph of the city's neighborhoods as recently as the 1960s, and the lack of trees will be striking. In fact, when Nikita Khrushchev visited San Francisco in 1959, he reportedly commented on the city's beauty but noted the remarkable lack of trees.

Things began to change in the late 1960s and 1970s when San Francisco (a center of the growing environmental movement) began city-sponsored street tree plantings in the neighborhoods. City arborists involved with the new program had to learn, through trial and (frequently) error, which trees would thrive in San Francisco's unique climate and topography. Early tree-planting efforts focused on a very few trees (ficus, blackwood acacia, myoporum, and others) selected for their rapid growth rates and tolerance of coastal conditions. Unfortunately, many of these fast-growing trees quickly developed into "green monsters" that buckled sidewalks, crowded narrow street setbacks, and (unforgivable in San Francisco) blocked views.

In 1981, things took a turn for the worse, as a municipal budget cut eliminated tree-planting programs in most of the city's neighborhoods. The city's tree-hugging residents responded in a typically San Franciscan fashion: they formed Friends of the Urban Forest, a volunteer-based nonprofit organization, to step into the breach and continue the greening of San Francisco. One of the country's oldest urban forestry organizations, this group conducts weekly Saturday morning programs in which residents and volunteers collaborate to plant and care for street trees. In addition to the energy and enthusiasm of its volunteers, Friends of the Urban Forest offers a growing expertise in recommending tree species appropriate for the city.

That expertise is important because of the unique geographic and climatic conditions that make San Francisco a challenging environment for trees. The city's climate is typically Mediterranean, with cool, wet winters and a long, cool dry season; the average high temperature in July is only 14° Fahrenheit higher than in January. The city's location at the Golden Gate, a gap in California's coastal range, adds even more unusual weather patterns. The summertime contrast between the cool, moist offshore air rushing through that gap and the warmer air rising from California's inland valleys creates the city's famous fog, as well as the sustained winds that make San Francisco the real Windy City. If this weren't enough, the city's topography creates further variations. The western neighborhoods closest to the ocean have the most wind and fog and, being built on former sand dunes, the sandiest (nutrient-poor) soils. The eastern, bay-facing neighborhoods are much sunnier, have better soils, and are less windy because they are sheltered by the city's hills.

The city's manmade environment also contributes to a unique environment for trees. San Francisco is the most densely populated U.S. city west of Manhattan, with little room for grassy medians or lawns. As a result, the city's street trees are almost always planted in small cuts in the city's sidewalks, in compacted soil that many trees cannot tolerate. In addition, narrow streets and overhead wires often leave no room for large tree canopies. Finally, San Franciscans love their views, so when it comes to a choice between tall trees and ocean or bay views, the trees often lose out.

Thus San Francisco's trees have to be able to handle lots of cement, driving wind, foggy summers, 7 months a year without rain, and attacks from view–conscious residents—hardly a place for maples and beeches. But through decades of trial and error, San Franciscans have discovered trees from around the world that thrive in this unique environment. This book introduces those trees to you.

FRIENDS OF THE URBAN FOREST

Until 1981, the planting of street trees in San Francisco was a purely municipal affair. If you wanted a tree in front of your house (or even if you didn't, for that matter), you waited for the city to plant one. You could do it yourself, but the prospect of cutting through the ubiquitous cement and dodging underground utility pipes and wires was enough to discourage most people from planting on their own. In 1981, however, a budget crisis caused the city to stop planting trees in most of San Francisco's neighborhoods. The city's tree-hugging residents responded in a typically San Franciscan fashion: they formed Friends of the Urban Forest (FUF), a volunteer-based nonprofit organization, to step into the breach and continue the greening of San Francisco.

Since 1981, FUF has planted almost 35,000 trees on the streets of San Francisco. Almost every Saturday morning, rain or shine, FUF conducts a neighborhood tree planting in which FUF's volunteers and staff join local residents to plant anywhere from 40 to over 200 trees in one of the city's neighborhoods. It is wonderful to experience the community spirit of these neighborhood plantings, as barren streets are transformed overnight and neighbors help their neighbors put the trees in the ground, often meeting one another for the first time.

With all its success in street tree planting, FUF is increasingly focused on tree care—the group now provides tree pruning and tree care visits for all its trees after 18 months and 3 years, with a goal of caring for all FUF trees through 5 years. Education is also an important part of the organization's mission. Over the years, FUF has helped San Franciscans learn which trees are right for the city's unique conditions. Many of the trees now common on the streets of San Francisco were experimental trees that FUF tested through trial and error over the past 20+ years.

I am a big fan of this organization, so here's a little plug: to volunteer or to donate, or just to learn more, go to FUF's website at www.fuf.net.

BAILEY'S ACACIA

This Australian native is the harbinger of spring in San Francisco. It is the earliest tree to flower, putting out brilliant yellow blossoms in January. (As a native of northern New York, I still find it jarring to associate January with spring.) The tree is

LOCATION: 236 Ashbury St./Fell St. near the Golden Gate Park panhandle; also at 1700 block of Fulton St. near Masonic Ave.; 500 Urbano Dr./Borica St. in the OMI neighborhood

popular for its attractive, feathery, blue–gray foliage, although the 'Purpurea' variety has lavender new growth. Bailey's acacia is one of the fastest growing San Francisco street trees, quickly reaching 20–30 feet in both height and width. Like most fast–growing trees, however, it is short lived, rarely surviving longer than 25 years. Known as "Cootamundra wattle" in Australia, this plant is native to a small area near the town of Cootamundra in New South Wales. It is a woody shrub in the wild, but it can be trained to grow as a tree.

BLACKWOOD ACACIA

LOCATION: 1 Northwood/Montecito in Westwood Park; also at 740 Masonic Ave./Hayes St.; many examples on Fell St. bordering the Golden Gate Park panhandle

One of the largest of San Francisco's street trees (to 40 feet in height, much higher under ideal conditions), black–wood acacia is also one of the most common—it was planted heavily throughout the city during the 1960s and 1970s, so many large, mature specimens are now found citywide. The tree is evergreen, with dark brown bark and dense gray–green "leaves" 3–5 inches long that actually are not leaves but enlarged leaf stalks called phyllodes. (Botanists believe that phyllodes are a moisture–preserving adapta–tion to a dry climate.) In February and March, the tree produces an abundance of globular, pale yellow flowers that put out a great deal of pollen.

Blackwood acacia is well adapted to San Francisco's coastal climate and will grow (rapidly) almost anywhere on city streets, as it is not afraid of sidewalks. In fact, just the opposite is true—this tree's aggressive roots will crack and lift sidewalks, which explains why in recent years it has been planted less frequently. Nevertheless, this is a good choice where a large, fast–growing tree is desired.

Blackwood acacia is native to the forests of southeastern Australia and Tasmania. It has always been an important timber tree in its native zone—the tree's hard wood made strong boomerangs, clubs, and shields for Australia's aboriginal people.

CALIFORNIA BUCKEYE

LOCATION: 2694 McAllister St./Willard St. near the USF campus. This is one of the most famous street trees in San Francisco. The tree is next to a very large California bay *(Umbellularia californica),* another California native. Also at 124 Lower Terrace/Levant St. in the Upper Market neighborhood.

ters of white flowers in May and June. One or two pear-shaped fruits are formed on each flower cluster, and inside each fruit's leathery jacket is a seed with a shiny brown coat. The tree's light green leaves are divided into five to seven leaflets, which drop in July unless summer water is provided.

Native Americans crushed this tree's poisonous seeds and added them to dammed-up streams to stupefy fish, making them easy to catch. (Today it is not unusual to find colonies of California buckeyes growing around old Indian campgrounds.)

This is a true San Francisco native, existing within the city limits before the arrival of Europeans. The California buckeye is also one of the state's most beautiful native trees, growing to 20 feet in height on wind-protected sites in the dry slopes and canyons of the coastal range and Sierra foothills. The tree produces showy long-lasting clus-

You can view a spectacular California buckeye at 2694 McAllister St., near the University of San Francisco campus. The tree was scheduled for removal in 1999 in connection with new construction on the lot, but after a neighborhood outcry, plans for the house were changed to build around, and preserve, the tree.

PEPPERMINT WILLOW

LOCATION: 3456 22d St./Fair Oaks St. in the Mission; also at 83 Stanyan St./Geary Blvd. in the Richmond; 214 Pierce St./Haight St. in the lower Haight-Ashbury. The 3 blocks surrounding St. John the Evangelist Church in Glen Park (St. Mary's Ave., Marsily St., and Bosworth St.) are lined with dozens of specimens.

This evergreen tree takes its common name from the distinctive minty smell of its leaves when crushed. Unlike most of San Francisco's Australian trees, which are from the east coast of that continent, the peppermint willow is from western Australia, near Perth. With luck, the tree can take on a graceful weeping form with its narrow willow–like leaves. But it is unpredictable in its growth pattern, particularly in windy locations—not surprisingly, flexuosa is Latin for "bending" or "curving."

The tree has small, inconspicuous white flowers that bloom in May and June. The ¼–inch seed capsules form in late summer and often persist on the tree from year to year. Peppermint willows grow rapidly, reaching 25–30 feet. The tree is a member of the myrtle family, related to eucalyptus, melaleuca, and bottlebrush trees. (Related species of plants belong to one genus, and related genera belong to one family.) The myrtles are a large family (Myrtaceae) composed of over 4,500 species. Typically, they grow in tropical and semitropical parts of the world, and—like the peppermint willow—their leaves often contain volatile aromatic oils.

BUNYA-BUNYA

Like its relative the Norfolk Island pine, the bunya–bunya has a distinctive silhouette. As with other members of the *Araucaria* genus, the tree's branches are spaced evenly along the trunk in whorls, giving the tree a symmetrical look. Bunya–bunyas are large trees, often reaching 80 feet, and mature trees develop a characteristic rounded crown. The glossy green leaves are lance shaped, sharply pointed, and spirally arranged on branches. The tree is native to the Bunya Mountains of Queensland in northern Australia.

Perhaps the most unusual feature of the bunya–bunya is its football–sized cone, which can weigh 10–15 pounds (the record is held by a 17–pounder). The cones, which set only every 3 years, are produced high in the tree's canopy and can cause serious injury when they fall. Each cone produces 50 to 100 large edible seeds, or bunya nuts. The nuts were a food source for Queensland's aborigines. When the cones set, the aborigines put aside their tribal differences and feasted. They headed for the Bunya Mountains, where each tribe owned particular trees. (Visitors to Bunya Mountains National Park can still see the notches that were carved into the

LOCATION: 201 Vicente St./Wawona St. in West Portal. This is one of the most spectacular trees in San Francisco, and a rare species in San Francisco. There is also a bunya-bunya in front of Chez Panisse restaurant in Berkeley, at 1517 Shattuck Ave.

trees to facilitate climbing for the harvest.)

Bunya nuts are still eaten today and are a delicacy in Australia. They can be eaten raw or roasted, and the nuts' flour can be used to make breads and cakes.

NORFOLK ISLAND PINE

LOCATION: 98 Lakewood Ave./Fairfield Way in the OMI neighborhood; also at 606 Ellis St./Hyde St. in the Tenderloin; 266 Pacheco St./Marcela Ave. in Forest Hill

There is no mistaking this tree. You may know it as the perfectly symmetrical, Christmas tree–like potted houseplant sold in discount stores and nurseries. It is equally distinctive in the landscape, maintaining its perfect pyramid-shaped symmetry with whorls of regularly spaced branches as it grows to heights of 100 feet (to 200 feet in its native habitat). The Norfolk Island pine's precise design never varies: the branches are in horizontal layers, equally spaced from one another; the layers generally have the same number of radiating branches; and in each layer the branches are the same length. The result is a unique, striking pagoda-like effect.

Despite its name, Norfolk Island pine is not a pine at all—it is a member of a small family of Southern Hemisphere conifers that also includes other trees of ornamental interest, such as the monkey puzzle tree (*Araucaria araucana*) and the bunya-bunya tree (*Araucaria bidwillii*). The light green overlapping needles are soft to the touch and grow densely on the branches, creating a cylindrical appearance. Mature trees bear spherical cones 3–5 inches long.

Araucaria heterophylla is native only to Norfolk Island, a remote, 3 by 5–mile island in the South Pacific, east of Australia and north of New Zealand. The island was discovered and claimed in 1774 by Captain James Cook, who hoped that the tall, straight trees would provide masts for Great Britain's Royal Navy. (In 1856, Great Britain forcibly resettled the residents of Pitcairn Island—the descendants of the famous mutineers from the HMS *Bounty*—to Norfolk Island, and today about half the island's population of 2,500 are descendants of the Pitcairners.)

STRAWBERRY TREE

LOCATION: an *Arbutus* 'Marina' at 1783 10th Ave./Noriega St. in the Sunset; many examples in the blocks nearby; many small examples on Plymouth Ave. between Ocean Ave. and Southwood Dr. in the Westwood Park neighborhood

This broadleaf evergreen tree is one of very few trees to flower during the fall, at which time the tree becomes covered with clusters of small cream-colored lanterns resembling lilies-of-the-valley. The tree takes its common name from the fruits that follow—round, red, strawberry-like fruits that are edible but mealy and unpleasant tasting. (The species name, *unedo*, is from the Latin phrase *unem edo*, "I eat [only] one.") The fruit is attractive to birds, however. The tree has beautiful, reddish, peeling bark, not unlike the Pacific madrone (*Arbutus menziesii*), to which it is closely related. The attractive, dark green leaves, 2–3 inches long, resemble bay leaves.

The strawberry tree is well adapted to San Francisco's climate and makes an excellent street tree (it ranks #5 among San Francisco's most frequently planted street trees). It is native to southern Europe and southwest Ireland. (I find it interesting that this tree from the Mediterranean is also found in southwest Ireland—an indication that the tree once ranged over a wider area of Europe, but was pushed south by the Ice Age, trapping one population in the area near Cork,

Ireland.) The Portuguese call this tree *medronho*, which is also the name of the strong liqueur they distill from its fruits.

The 'Marina' variety of this tree is a hybrid, with larger leaves, rosy pink flowers, and an interesting San Francisco history. It was introduced into the nursery trade by the Saratoga Horticultural Foundation in 1984. The Foundation took cuttings from a tree in the late Victor Reiter's garden on Stanyan St. in San Francisco. Reiter, a renowned horticulturist and plant breeder (see the following page) acquired his plant in 1933 from a

cutting of a boxed specimen in San Francisco's Strybing Arboretum. Strybing purchased the tree from the closing sale of Western Nursery on Lombard St. in the Marina District of San Francisco—hence the 'Marina' name. The nursery is thought to have taken cuttings from trees that were sent from Europe for display in San Francisco's 1917 Panama–Pacific International Exposition, one of which eventually became *Arbutus* 'Marina'. The largest known *Arbutus* 'Marina' in existence is a 50-foot specimen planted in 1944 in Reiter's garden.

The strawberry tree is one of the few trees to display flowers and mature fruits at the same time.

VICTOR REITER'S

Secret Garden

Nowhere else in the city but the west side of Stanyan Street in Cole Valley would you see a rare yellow New Zealand Christmas tree (page 69) in front of an even rarer *Leptospermum* (so rare that even the experts cannot identify it), up the street from a rare magnolia tree. These trees are a hint of something special tucked behind these houses—a secret garden associated with one of San Francisco's most renowned plant experts.

Victor Reiter moved to 1195 Stanyan St. in 1926. One of the founders of the California Horticultural Society, Reiter was San Francisco's most famous grower, hybridizer, and collector of plants and trees, responsible for introducing many hybridized varieties of plants to the world, but perhaps best known for the creation of many different varieties of fuchsias. Reiter also helped introduce to the world one of San Francisco's most popular trees, *Arbutus* 'Marina' (page 19). During the early 1930s, Reiter began building a commercial nursery on the property behind his home. He bought parcels from the Sutro family (descendants of Adolf Sutro, the San Francisco mayor) in a several-acre area between Stanyan St., Woodland Ave., and Sutro Forest. The nursery lasted until 1963, but Reiter continued to plant and care for the specimen trees on the property until his death. Amazingly, the garden still survives—forgotten and neglected, perhaps—but it survives. It is private property, still in the family (owned by Victor's widow, Carla, who continues to live in the family home on Stanyan St.), but if you peer over the fence at the south end of Woodland Ave., you'll catch a glimpse of it, and you can also see a bit of the garden over the fence on Stanyan St. near Rivoli St. The garden is most beautiful in January, when blooms are produced on two striking trees: one of the city's largest michelias *(Michelia doltsopa)*, with spectacular white flowers; and a large, beautiful, pink-and-white Campbell's magnolia *(Magnolia campbellii)*. The garden also has what is probably the world's largest *Arbutus* 'Marina,' most likely the genetic parent of the nursery stock now sold throughout California.

LEMON BOTTLEBRUSH

This tree has striking clusters of bright red bottle-brush–like flowers, which appear in waves throughout the year but seem to peak in May. The flowers, which attract hummingbirds, are actually clusters of hundreds of long red stamens (the male

LOCATION: 4022–4024 23rd St./Noe St. in Noe Valley; also at 437–469 Arkansas St./19th St. (several trees) on Potrero Hill

organ of the flower). In fact, the genus name *Callistemon* is from the Greek *kalos* (beautiful) and *stemon* (stamen). Flowers are followed by small woody seed capsules that can persist for years, embedded in the bark of the branches after the flowers have fallen. Crushed leaves have a lemony scent— hence the common name—and the fragrance is an easy way to distinguish this tree from its relative, the weeping bottlebrush (*Callistemon viminalis*). In its native Australia this plant is a large shrub, but it can easily be trained as a single or multitrunked tree (rarely taller than 20 feet).

The lemon bottlebrush is hardy and well adapted to the Bay Area's climate and conditions. It makes an excellent street tree and is a good choice for locations under utility wires.

WEEPING BOTTLEBRUSH

The weeping bottlebrush is less common in San Francisco than the lemon bottlebrush, perhaps because its red flowers are not as showy. It has a graceful, pendulous branching structure and is larger than the lemon bottlebrush, capable of growing to 30 to 35 feet. Like its cousin, however, it is hardy, thrives in almost any soil conditions, and is native to Australia.

LOCATION: 332–334 Steiner St./ Page St. in the lower Haight-Ashbury; also at 870 Chenery St./Lippard Ave. in Glen Park; parking lot behind 498 Castro St./18th St. in the Castro; 1370 Sanchez St./27th St. in Noe Valley

WILD LILAC

Ceanothus, or wild lilac, is an evergreen shrub found primarily in the western United States and Mexico. California alone is home to over thirty–five species of *Ceanothus*. The plants are notable for their attractive flower clusters, typically in shades of blue ranging from deep indigo to pale blue, although a few varieties have white flowers. Horticulturists have contributed to the diversity of *Ceanothus*, producing an array of cultivars in a wide range of colors, forms, and sizes. *Ceanothus* 'Ray Hartman' is the most popular cultivar in San Francisco and the only one used as a street tree. It can grow to 20 feet, with showy, dense, medium blue flower clusters and glossy, deep green leaves 2–3 inches long. This cultivar's parentage is thought to include *Ceanothus arboreus* from Southern California's Channel Islands.

LOCATION:
Corner of Liberty
and Sanchez Sts.
in the Castro

ATLAS CEDAR; CEDAR OF LEBANON

LOCATION: 431 Yerba Buena Ave./Monterey Blvd. near St. Francis Wood; also at 15 Woodland Ave./Parnassus Ave. in Parnassus Heights

The Atlas cedar, native to the Atlas Mountains of Algeria and Morocco, was once thought to be a unique species. But after a 1996 study by botanists in the eastern Mediterranean and North Africa, it is now considered a subspecies of *Cedrus libani* (cedar of Lebanon). However, this popular landscaping tree will likely continue to be sold by nurseries as Atlas cedar for some time. Like all cedars, this tree bears needles in tufted clusters. The needles are normally a bluish green, although the popular 'Glauca' variety has attractive silvery blue needles. The distinctive barrel-shaped cones sit upright on top of the branches and can take up to 2 years to mature. In North Africa, cedar oil has long been used as a folk remedy for various ills, and the ancient Egyptians used it for embalming. Too big to be ideal as a street tree, the Atlas cedar can be a striking specimen in a lawn or garden.

DEODAR CEDAR

LOCATION: 625 St. Francis Blvd./San Anselmo Ave. in St. Francis Wood; also at 183 Edgewood Ave./Belmont Ave. in Parnassus Heights

This native of the Himalayas takes its name from the Sanskrit *devadara*, meaning "tree of the gods." A favorite in the western United States, particularly in Seattle and the Northwest, the deodar cedar has a distinctive pyramidal silhouette, especially when young; older trees develop a graceful drooping shape. The tree is large, reaching 40–60 feet, and needs room to be shown at its best—most of San Francisco's deodar cedars are in the city's western neighborhoods, where yards are larger. The tree's stiff, needle-like leaves are about 2 inches long and borne in dense clusters that are pendulous at the end (this is an easy way to distinguish the tree from *Cedrus atlantica*). Male banana–shaped catkins produce clouds of yellow pollen in early spring. The bluish green female cones are 3–5 inches long and egg shaped; after 2 years they shatter and release little seeds with papery wings.

CAROB

LOCATION: 957 Cole St./Parnassus Ave. in Cole Valley; a rare female tree with pods at 3733–3735 20th St./Dolores St. in the Mission

This is a tree with biblical roots. It is said that the foot–long, brown, leathery fruit pods of the carob tree were the "locusts" that St. John the Baptist survived on in the wilderness in the gospel of Mark. The pods are also thought to be the "husks" that tempted the prodigal son in the New Testament parable.

Rich in sugar and protein, the carob's pods can be milled to a fine powder for use as a chocolate substitute. Within the pods, the carob seeds are of remarkably uniform weight, and ancient Mediterranean civilizations used them as a unit of measure to weigh gems and other precious substances (the Arabic word for the carob seed was *quirat*, whence our word "carat"). You will rarely see the pods or seeds of the carob in San Francisco, because only female trees produce them (11 months after pollination), and the females are rarely planted on city streets.

The carob is a native of the eastern Mediterranean. It grows to 30 feet, with a dense, rounded crown. This is a tree to plant for its foliage—the glossy, dark green leaves are beautiful and distinctive, with each compound leaf divided into four to ten round leaflets. Small, inconspicuous red flowers form in spring. Not surprising, given its desert origin, the carob is very drought tolerant. A drawback: carobs have extremely invasive roots, and mature trees will cause significant sidewalk damage.

CAMPHOR

LOCATION: 404 Ashbury St./Oak St. in the Haight-Ashbury; also at 3828 Cesar Chavez St./ Dolores St. in Noe Valley; 418 Union St./Kearny St. on Telegraph Hill

Take a leaf from this tree and crush it, letting the pungent aroma of mothballs rise to your nose. Extracting camphor from the twigs, leaves, and wood of this tree has been practiced in Asia for over 1,000 years. The substance was once thought to be useful against a variety of ills, including epilepsy and heart problems; now it is used primarily for lotions to relieve itching and superficial pain.

In addition to its olfactory charms, the camphor tree is also distinctive for the pale green color of its oval, 3–4-inch leaves, which form a broadly rounded crown. The tree's aggressive roots make it a poor sidewalk tree, but given some room to spread out it will grow to 50 feet, occasionally much higher under the right conditions. Camphor trees are one of the most common ornamental trees in suburban California, where lawns and grassy sidewalk medians provide room for them to grow.

The camphor is a close botanical relative of another aromatic tree, the Grecian laurel or sweet bay. Camphors are native to China and Japan.

GIANT DRACAENA; CABBAGE PALM

LOCATION: the Main Post of the San Francisco Presidio (many other examples nearby); also across from 1963 9th Ave./Pacheco St. in the Sunset; common in blocks nearest the ocean in the Sunset and Richmond neighborhoods

This New Zealand native has a distinctive look: an open canopy punctuated by bursts of long, narrow, sword-like leaves. Perhaps because it looks like a palm, the giant dracaena is often grouped with palms in nurseries, although it is more closely related botanically to agaves and yuccas. The tree produces large clusters of fragrant, small white flowers in April and May, followed by small white berries in the fall. The Maoris of New Zealand had many uses for this tree, eating the inner leaves and stems as a vegetable and using the dried leaves for baskets, footwear, and bird snares. This is one of the very few trees that will thrive in the blocks closest to the ocean in San Francisco, where the sandy soil, unrelenting wind, salt spray, and fog cause less hardy trees to fail. (I've often thought of the giant dracaena as the unofficial municipal tree of Pacifica and Daly City, San Francisco's wind-swept neighbors to the south.) The tree's "tough to kill" qualities also make it a good choice for gardeners without green thumbs.

Corymbia citriodora (formerly *Eucalyptus citriodora*)

LEMON-SCENTED GUM

Many people consider this tree the most beautiful of our Australian imports, and it is not hard to see why. The tree's most striking feature is its smooth bark, which can vary from solid white, pale yellow, or pink, to a beautiful mottle of all three colors. The tree has a graceful, narrow, weeping structure; the long (3–7 inches) and narrow light green leaves have a strong lemon scent when crushed.

The oil of the lemon–scented gum has a high citronella content and is popular with aromatherapists and in folk medicine, where it is used to treat colds and other pulmonary problems. The oil is also used as an antiseptic, and it makes an excellent insect repellent.

The lemon–scented gum occurs naturally only in the northern Australian state of Queensland, but the tree fares well in many parts of Africa, Brazil, and India. It is also common in California, but in San Francisco it seems to be limited to warmer neighborhoods such as the Mission.

LOCATION: median strip of Mission St. near 14th St. in the Mission

Corymbia ficifolia (formerly *Eucalyptus ficifolia*)

RED FLOWERING GUM

LOCATION: Median strip of Van Ness Ave. between Grove and McAllister Sts., with City Hall's dome in the background. San Francisco has reputedly the country's largest red flowering gum—on the east side of Junipero Serra Ave. between St. Francis and Monterey Blvds.

The red flowering gum is one of San Francisco's most common and most striking trees. It is easily recognizable by its clusters of brilliant red, pink, orange, or white flowers, which can bloom at any time but are at their peak in July. This tree cannot be easily reproduced from cuttings, and when the tree is reproduced from seed, the flower color rarely matches that of the parent tree. Large, smooth, and woody seed capsules (they look like the bowl of a pipe) form after the flowering and hang onto the tree for many months— often until the next year's flowers are in bloom. The tree is evergreen, with dark green, glossy, leathery leaves and a dense, round crown that grows rap-idly to 30–40 feet. Red gums are well adapted to San Francisco's climate (the country's largest red gum is within San Francisco city limits), and they can be counted on to thrive in most areas of the city. If you want a large tree, this is a great choice—but it is not recommended under utility wires or if you are concerned about your sidewalk! The native range of the red flowering gum is a very small area (approximately 1 square kilometer) in western Australia, south of Perth.

The flowers of the red gum side by side with the bowl-shaped seed capsules from the previous year.

ENGLISH HAWTHORN

This tree is a "parrot magnet" in my neighborhood. Every July and August, when the tree's fruits ripen, twenty to forty birds from the flock of wild parrots in San Francisco leave their roost near Telegraph Hill and descend on the English hawthorns in my neighbors' backyards, feasting on the fruits. (See story on the following page.) Although it has long been cultivated, this deciduous tree is native to Europe and North Africa. Different varieties of English hawthorn have red or white flowers, followed by small red fruits that persist throughout the winter (unless the birds eat them first). As the name suggests, this tree has thorny branches, which northern Europeans historically put to good use. Long before the use of barbed wire, this was the hedgerow tree of England and northern Europe, marking property lines and keeping neighbors' sheep out of owners' fields ("hawthorn" is Old English for "hedge-thorn"). In San Francisco, the English hawthorn is a good small ornamental, typically 15–20 feet tall, and excellent for locations under utility wires. The most commonly planted cultivar in San Francisco is 'Paul's Scarlet,' which has showy, dark pink, double-flowered blooms.

LOCATION: 939 Castro St./22nd St. in Noe Valley; 31 Belmont St./Willard St. in Parnassus Heights; common throughout the Forest Hill neighborhood

San Francisco's WILD PARROTS

and Their Favorite Trees

A flock of wild parrots—estimated at seventy-five birds or more—has taken up residence in the city. They roost in a park near the Embarcadero Center, although a second breeding spot has been observed in the Presidio. The birds are red-masked conures, native to Ecuador and Peru, the offspring of pet birds that escaped in the late 1980s and early 1990s. Brilliant green with red heads, the parrots have become a tourist attraction in San Francisco, complete with their own website at www.pelicanmedia.org/wildparrots.html.

During breeding season, the parrots like to nest in Canary Island palm trees. When the fronds break off the trunk, a small hole or indentation is often created. The parrots can turn these places into perfect nesting holes. The palms also give the parrots a high perch with good visibility for watching for hawks, their most common predator in the city.

Most of the year, the parrots rarely wander outside the northeast quadrant of the city, ranging from the Ferry Building to the eastern edge of the Presidio. Early in July the parrots make their annual summer trek to the Cole Valley and Parnassus Heights neighborhoods—and depart just as punctually at the end of August.

Why do they visit only in July and August? The plum trees on the streets of this neighborhood are one reason. Even though the city discourages fruit-bearing trees on the streets, many trees in Parnassus Heights are laden with ripe plums in July and August—an irresistible delicacy for the parrots, which perch in the trees, methodically grabbing the plums and eating them from their claws. An even bigger draw for the parrots are the backyard English hawthorn trees, whose fruit also ripens in July and August.

Stroll through Parnassus Heights, ideally early in the morning in July. The parrots typically travel in flocks of ten to as many as forty birds, so if these colorful loudmouths are in the neighborhood, they'll be hard to miss. You'll probably hear them before you see them, as their raucous cries can be heard from blocks away.

LAVALLE HAWTHORN

LOCATION: 3875 21st St./Castro St. in the Castro; also at 2134 9th Ave./Mendosa Ave. in Forest Hill; 2 Belmont Ave./Edgewood Ave. in Parnassus Heights

Of the three main hawthorn species growing in San Francisco, the Lavalle hawthorn is, to my eye, the most attractive. But for reasons I don't understand, it is also by far the least common of the three. This tree pleases in all seasons. In late spring it produces dense masses of white blooms, although for some people the fragrance is an acquired taste. Summer brings glossy, dark green leaves and brilliant red fruit resembling tiny apples (like true apples, hawthorns are members of the rose family). In most areas, autumn generates showy bronze and crimson foliage, but fall color is usually disappointing in San Francisco's mild climate. Winter reveals the stately branching structure of the tree (unusual for a hawthorn), while the red fruits persist almost until spring. We have the French to thank for this tree, which originated as a hybrid in the Segrez Arboretum in France in 1880. The Latin name for the tree recognizes Pierre Lavallèe, the arboretum's founder.

WASHINGTON THORN

LOCATION: 45 Hartford St./17th St. in the Castro; also at 247 28th St./Church St. in Noe Valley; many examples on Stoneman St. between Manchester and Folsom Sts. in Bernal Heights

The Washington thorn is the only North American native among the city's three hawthorns; it is native to the southeastern United States, from Virginia to Alabama and west to Missouri. It is also the last to flower, its white blooms not arriving until June. Although it resembles the English hawthorn, the Washington thorn has larger leaves (2–3 inches) and longer thorns (1–3 inches) than its European relative. Like most hawthorns, it has glossy red, pea–sized fruit that persists during the winter. The foliage turns mixes of orange and scarlet in fall, although, like the Lavalle hawthorn, fall color for this tree is muted in San Francisco. This is a good choice for a site where a small tree is needed, because it rarely exceeds 20 feet in height. Washington thorns are not at their best near the coast, but they can thrive in San Francisco's warmer eastern neighborhoods.

MONTEREY CYPRESS

LOCATION: In front of McLaren Lodge, near the corner of Stanyan and Fell Sts. in Golden Gate Park. During the holidays this tree is covered with colorful lights, making it San Francisco's unofficial Christmas tree. Another beautiful example is at the corner of Cedro Ave. and Mercedes Way in the OMI neighborhood.

This evergreen conifer is one of San Francisco's most common trees, but you almost never find it on the street– the tree is too large for most street tree plantings, growing quickly to 40 feet and reaching 100 feet under ideal conditions. Monterey cypress is much more common in the city's parks, where together with the Monterey pine and blue gum it has become dominant. This tree is widely cultivated throughout California as an ornamental, and it is also popular in Europe, Australia, and New Zealand.

Monterey cypress has a distinctive pyramid–like shape when young. The tree develops real character and beauty as it ages, particularly near the ocean, where the winds sculpt and distort its shape. The most famous example is the "lone cypress" that has become a symbol of Pebble Beach, California.

Only two native stands of Monterey cypress exist. One is at Point Lobos State Park (3 miles south of Carmel), and one is in Pebble Beach (appropriately enough at Cypress Point). This limited natural range is the smallest of any tree in California. In the wild, Monterey cypress is normally dependent on fire to cause its cones to open and the seeds to disperse. Some cones may open on very hot summer days, which explains why the tree does not self–propagate in San Francisco, which has neither fires in its parks nor many hot summer days! Many of the trees planted in the late 1800s when San Francisco's parks were established are now reaching the end of their life spans of 100+ years. The city is gradually culling older trees and planting new ones, to establish a more natural forest with trees of various ages.

HOPSEED

LOCATION: southeast corner of Bush and Larkin Sts. on Nob Hill; also at 140 Belgrave Ave./Stanyan St. and 251 Frederick St./Downey St., both in Cole Valley

The hopseed is a shrub by nature (in fact, it is often used as a hedge), but it can easily be pruned to become a tree. This evergreen has narrow leaves that grow to 3–4 inches and form a dense canopy. The popular 'Purpurea' variety, which was introduced to the world by San Francisco's Strybing Arboretum, has bronzy green leaves that look purplish from a distance. Insignificant flowers in spring produce papery, ornamental seed capsules in late summer. The hopseed is an excellent tree below overhead wires, as it rarely grows higher than 15 feet. It is also a hardy tree, tolerant of poor soil, wind, and fog. The hopseed is native to many warm and tropical regions worldwide, including Australia, South America, the American Southwest, and Hawaii. In Hawaii, where it is known as 'a'ali'i in the native language, it is one of the first "colonizing" plants to grow in lava beds, and the leaves and papery seeds of the tree are used in leis. Australian pioneers used the tree's seeds as a substitute for hops in beer making, hence the tree's common name.

BRONZE LOQUAT

Bronze loquats are recognizable by the coppery bronze color of their new foliage, which eventually fades to green, giving the trees an attractive two-tone appearance for much of the year. The tree, which grows to 25–30 feet, has creamy white flower clusters from March to May, but it rarely bears fruit. A related variety of loquat, *Eriobotrya japonica,* is also found in the Bay Area (but more often in back-yards) and bears edible, orange–yellow fruit 1–2 inches in length. The bronze loquat is native to Taiwan; its edible relative is from China and southern Japan.

LOCATION: 1575 10th Ave./ Lawton St. in the Sunset; also at 1241 7th Ave./Lincoln Way in the Sunset

COCKSPUR CORAL TREE

The cockspur coral tree is likely to be better known to readers from Southern California, where it is common. San Francisco is outside the normal range of this warmth–loving tree. In fact, I am aware of only one example of this tree in San Francisco: a large and healthy specimen in a wind–protected spot in Dolores Heights. (The best time to visit this tree is in late June and July, when it is in full bloom.) Cockspur coral trees are native to southern Brazil, Uruguay, and north–ern Argentina. *Crista-galli* is Latin for "cock's comb," which the distinctive showy pink flowers resemble—they are like nothing else you will find in a Bay Area tree. In Argentina, children call the flowers *patitos* (ducklings), because they float like little ducks when dropped in water.

LOCATION: 366 Cumberland St./Sanchez St. in Dolores Heights. This warmth-loving tree found a niche in a wind-sheltered, sunny spot of the city.

BLUE GUM

LOCATION: parking lot, Main Post of the San Francisco Presidio; also several large specimens at 1661 Octavia St./Bush St. (see the following page); across the street from 2150 Fell St./Shrader St. near the Golden Gate Park panhandle

This Australian native is likely the most common nonnative tree in California. The blue gum was introduced to California in 1856, and the fast-growing tree was planted extensively by pioneers hoping to make a fast buck from timber plantations (a mistake, as it turned out—the wood of the blue gum is not well suited for sawn timber). The blue gum has since naturalized and become common in California—too common for some native plant enthusiasts, who push for its eradication. As one example, nearly all the 80+ acres of blue gums on Angel Island in San Francisco Bay were removed during the 1990s, many

of them by helicopter. Others (myself included) are not so doctrinaire; I associate eucalyptus with California and cannot imagine the state without them. The blue gum is one of our largest trees—its towering, cloud-like crown can reach 150–200 feet in ideal conditions (in its native Tasmania, the tree is known to reach 300 feet).

The leaves of the blue gums undergo an interesting change in shape as trees mature. The waxy juvenile leaves produced in the tree's early years are silvery blue and rounded, occurring in opposite pairs on the branch. The deep green adult leaves are sickle shaped, thick, and leathery, and hang vertically from the tree's branches. This makes them perfectly adapted to the California coast's dry but foggy summers—the leathery leaves retain moisture, and their vertical sickle shape causes the condensing fog to drip onto the ground, delivering moisture to the tree's roots. The bark sheds in long strips, creating an attractive striped mottling of greens and tans.

Blue gums are a major source of eucalyptus oil, which has disinfecting properties and is used in a number of products. The oil is extracted from the twigs and leaves of the tree. The tree is native to a very small range in Tasmania and southeastern Australia.

MARY ELLEN PLEASANT

and her Blue Gums

The row of mature blue gums *(Eucalyptus globulus)* at 1661 Octavia St./Bush St. in Pacific Heights was planted by Mary Ellen Pleasant, an African American woman often called the "Mother of Civil Rights in California." Pleasant, who owned a sprawling, thirty-room estate at this address, was born a slave in 1817. Subsequently granted her freedom, she spent many of her early years helping fugitive slaves escape the South. Pursued by the law, she headed to gold rush San Francisco in 1852, where with her business acumen she parlayed an inheritance from her first husband into an estimated $30 million fortune. She used her wealth to continue her efforts to support the rights of African Americans. Her house on this site has been referred to as the western terminus of the Underground Railway, which helped to bring fugitive slaves to freedom in pre–Civil War times. In 1868, long before the civil rights battles of the next century, Pleasant brought a lawsuit against two San Francisco cable car lines that had denied her the right to ride because of her race. Her suit ultimately went to the California Supreme Court, where she won the right for all African Americans to ride the streetcars.

Later in life, Mary Ellen Pleasant suffered tabloid-driven scandals and financial reverses. She died in San Francisco in 1904 and is buried in Napa's Tulocay Cemetery. All that is left of her opulent mansion is the row of blue gum eucalyptus she planted in front of her property on Octavia St. Set in the sidewalk amid these trees is a historical marker identifying the trees as something special—a part of San Francisco's history.

SILVER DOLLAR GUM

This evergreen has blue–green round or oval leaves and grows rapidly to 30–45 feet. The younger leaves have the rounder "silver dollar" shape and are often used (fresh or dry) in floral arrangements. Creamy white flowers bloom in clusters in the spring, although they are not very showy. Flowers are followed by greenish brown seed capsules that form in the summer and drop during winter storms. The bark is fibrous. The silver dollar gum is one of our largest street trees. It is native to Victoria and New South Wales in eastern Australia, where it is known as "red box" and is a valuable timber tree.

LOCATION: north side of Bryant St. near 7th St. in the SOMA neighborhood, with the modernist San Francisco jail in the background; also on the Sanchez St. median near Henry St. in the Castro

RED IRONBARK

Red ironbark is one of the largest commonly planted street trees in San Francisco—it can reach 80–90 feet in ideal conditions. The tree is easily recognized by its furrowed, nearly black bark and its narrow, grayish green leaves, which hang in a weeping habit in mature specimens. The tree has white, pink, or reddish flowers, but as with many eucalyptus, seedlings are often not true to their parent tree in flower color. The species name *sideroxylon* derives from the Greek *sideros* (iron) and *xylon* (wood)—a reference to the hardness of the timber, which in Australia is used for support beams and other applications requiring great strength. Red ironbark is native to New South Wales, Australia, where it often grows in stands with silver dollar gum (*Eucalyptus polyanthemos*), another common San Francisco tree.

LOCATION: 467 Pennsylvania Ave./20th St. on Potrero Hill; many examples on Cortland Ave. from Mission St. to Bonview Ave. in Bernal Heights

EUCALYPTUS

The eucalyptus is Australia's gift to California. Almost all the approximately 500 species of eucalyptus are from Australia, and an estimated 75 percent of the forest trees in Australia are eucalyptus. Although there is a lot of variety among the species in the very large genus, eucalypts (as they are known in Australia) also share many characteristics. All eucalyptus have a flower bud with a lid that comes off when the sexual parts inside are ready to receive pollinating insects—hence the genus name, which is from the Greek *eu* (well) and *kalypto* (to cover). The flowers are also characteristic—unlike many flowering trees, it is not the petals of eucalyptus that put on the show; instead, what you see in a eucalyptus flower are masses of long, thin stamens (the male, pollen-producing part of the flower). The leaves and twigs of most eucalyptus have aromatic oils that produce a characteristic fragrance when crushed.

Eucalyptus have adapted well to California's mild Mediterranean climate. In fact, they have become so common in California that many people don't realize that the trees are not native to the state. Some native-plant enthusiasts would like to eradicate the eucalyptus in California, but as a nonnative myself, I don't count myself among them. Like other immigrants, these trees have been around long enough and contributed enough to the California experience to have earned the right to stay. I find it hard to imagine the San Francisco Presidio, Golden Gate Park, or the Stanford University campus without them!

FICUS; INDIAN LAUREL FIG

LOCATION: 1049 Dolores St./24th St. in the Mission; also at 2150–2152 15th St./Sanchez St. in the Castro; the entire length of Potrero Ave. in the Mission

Until the late 1980s, ficus was probably the most heavily planted street tree in San Francisco, and rightly so, since no tree is better adapted to our urban conditions. It is not finicky about sidewalks, wind, or fog, and it grows vigorously almost everywhere in the city. The dense, brilliant green foliage of this tree and its round "tree-like" canopy create a welcome break from the gray of urban existence. But in recent years, problems with ficus as a street tree have emerged, particularly as the trees have matured. The roots of mature ficus are extremely invasive, causing sidewalks to buckle, and the dense foliage of the tree can block light and air (and views!). San Franciscans discovered another drawback to the ficus during the winter of 1990–1991, when a freak cold snap caused the temperature in the city to drop to the mid–20s. Thousands of ficus (which are native to Southeast Asia) died overnight. Berkeley's renowned Telegraph Ave., whose entire length until then was lined with ficus, lost every one. San Franciscans have since learned their lesson; you will still see lots of ficus in San Francisco, but you will not see many young specimens.

SHAMEL ASH; EVERGREEN ASH

LOCATION: 501 Masonic Ave./McAllister St. in the Western Addition; many examples on Noe St. between Market and 14th Sts. in the Castro

Shamel ash is one of the largest of the common San Francisco street trees. Vigorous, fast growing, and pest resistant, it seemed a great choice when the city began planting street trees in the 1950s and 1960s. Now it is rarely planted in San Francisco, because it is too large for the narrow setbacks in many parts of the city. Nevertheless, you will still see many beautiful mature specimens on the streets (unfortunately, even more that have been pruned too aggressively by owners who probably wish that they had something much more manageable). Typically evergreen in San Francisco's climate, the tree can reach 40 feet in 20 years, ultimately topping out at 70 feet. The leaves are divided into five to nine glossy, dark green leaflets about 4 inches long. Shamel ash is native to southern Mexico and Guatemala and is frequently planted as a street tree in Mexican cities. The tree has become an invasive pest in Hawaii.

AUSTRALIAN WILLOW

This evergreen Australian native has pendulous branches that make it look like a willow, although it is more closely related to citrus trees. Australian willows have an oval form and grow 20–30 feet tall, with a dense canopy of narrow, gray-green leaves. Flowers are inconspicuous, and the tree has smooth gray bark. This tree stands neglect better than most—it is very resistant to drought, disease, and pests. Australian willow is native to the dry interior of Australia (unlike most of our Aussie natives, which are from coastal regions). In its homeland, the tree is known as the "wilga" (a name probably derived from local aboriginal languages) and is a common shade tree near dusty farmhouses. The leaves have a mild analgesic effect—as a traditional folk remedy, chewed leaves were often used to stop toothaches. Another traditional use of this species among the aborigines was as a kind of narcotic; during ceremonies they smoked the dried leaves, which

LOCATION: 673–675 Guerrero St./22nd St. in the Mission; also on the 1700 block of Hayes St./Masonic Ave. in the Western Addition; 1400 block of 20th St./Texas St. on Potrero Hill

reportedly induced a "drowsiness and drunkenness." In modern-day San Francisco, Australian willow is used for its aesthetic rather than for any psychoactive properties—as an attractive ornamental that takes almost any kind of neglect.

GINKGO; MAIDENHAIR

Indeed, there is some controversy as to whether those ginkgos are truly native or were introduced by humans. Some botanists believe that the ginkgo was completely wiped out in the wild by the last Ice Age and that the species survived only in the temple gardens of ancient Asian peoples who cultivated it as a sacred tree.

LOCATION: 200 block of Eureka St./20th St. in the Castro; also at 1629 Dolores St./29th St. in the Mission; 494 and 498 Jackson St./ Montgomery St. in the financial district

Basque is an ancient and unique language of unknown origin, spoken only in a small area near the border between France and Spain and unrelated to any other living language. The ginkgo is aptly described as the "Basque of trees." It is thought to be the oldest surviving plant on earth, the sole remaining species of a now-vanished plant family that was common worldwide during the time of the dinosaurs more than 200 million years ago. Ginkgos survive in the wild only in a tiny area of remote eastern China.

In addition to its impressive pedigree, the ginkgo is a spectacular urban street tree, with a graceful but unique and unpredictable form, growing slowly to 50 feet or higher. Among the ginkgo's many distinctive features are its leaves, which have a beautiful and unique fan shape, with a notch in the center of the blade. Ginkgos are one of the last trees to leaf out in the spring, typically in mid–April. The leaves are spectacular in the fall, turning a monochromatic gold before dropping all at once in late November or early December. One advantage of the ginkgo is that, being an ancient tree, virtually extinct in the wild, many of its natural enemies have disappeared, leaving it relatively free from insect and disease problems. It tolerates poor soils and urban pollution well.

The ginkgo is also unique in that, unlike other broad-leaved trees, it is a gymnosperm—from the Greek *gymnos* (naked) and *sperma* (seed)—meaning that like conifers, its "fruits" are not fruits at all but naked seeds (individual seeds with fleshy seed coats). Female trees produce these nonfruit fruits that resemble small plums, but the seed coat decomposes at maturity, producing butyric acid (which smells like rancid butter) and *n*–hexanoic acid (said to smell like old gym socks).

When ginkgos lived in the wild, the funky odors likely attracted some form of animal that helped to disperse the seeds.

The ginkgo was first imported to Europe in 1730 by Dutch traders. The oldest specimen in the United States—in Philadelphia's Woodlands Cemetery—was brought from England in 1784. Ginkgos are extremely long-lived trees; a tree in Sendai, Japan, is over 1,200 years old.

SILK OAK

LOCATION: 601 Diamond St./23rd St. in Noe Valley; also at 3520 18th St./Valencia St. in the Mission

A large forest tree in its native Australia, the handsome silk oak is not an oak at all, but its beautifully grained, pale pinkish wood resembles oak. Australians make beautiful cabinets out of silk oaks; San Franciscans admire the trees for their ornamental value. The silk oak grows quickly to 50 feet and is recognizable by its graceful, fernlike, 6–12-inch compound leaves. If the tree receives enough heat in summer, it produces showy, 2–4-inch, bright orange flowers—you will almost never see the flowers in San Francisco, but they bloom beautifully 25 miles to the east in Walnut Creek and Concord.

Unique among San Francisco street trees, silk oaks belong to the Protea family, a group of trees and shrubs native to South Africa as well as Australia. The tree has become naturalized in Hawaii and southern Florida, reproducing so vigorously that it is considered an invasive pest. It is planted extensively in the tropics as a shade tree for coffee and tea plantations.

SWEETSHADE

This tree is entitled to at least one superlative among San Francisco's trees: it smells the best. The clusters of 1-inch, light yellow flowers have a long blooming season—from March to September—and the fragrance (reminiscent of orange blossoms) is amazing. Sweetshade's upright, dark green canopy is open and spare, with an almost twiggy look, even when the tree is healthy. The problem is that the tree is not often healthy in San Francisco's climate, since it does not tolerate wind or fog well. Sweetshade was planted heavily in San Francisco as an experimental tree during the 1990s—it was thought to be a good

LOCATION: 1230–1232 Castro St./24th St. in Noe Valley

alternative to Victorian box (*Pittosporum undulatum*), sharing the fragrant blossoms but without the messy fruit drop. However, it has proved disappointing as a street tree, particularly in the western half of the city, and surveys of street trees suggest that its survival rate in street plantings is low. This tree is much happier in its native Queensland and New South Wales, Australia, where it is known as "native frangipani."

San Francisco's

DOWN UNDER Connection

Australia and New Zealand make up only 5 percent of Earth's land mass, but they're much more important than that to San Francisco's urban forest. Of the city's 50 most frequently planted trees, Australia and New Zealand have contributed a total of 22 species.

Why are trees from such a small corner of the world so common in San Francisco? It's all about climate. Coastal regions in Australia and New Zealand have the same mild climate as San Francisco: rainy, mostly frost-free winters and long, mild summers. Their maritime conditions also mimic those of San Francisco—these are trees that in their native regions have become used to strong winds, salt spray, and sandy soils.

Eucalyptus, in particular, has really taken off as a California import. The blue gum (*Eucalyptus globulus*) and other eucalyptus species have become naturalized in the California countryside, where they are so common that many people assume they must be native trees. In San Francisco, blue gums are one of three "foundation trees" of Golden Gate Park, along with California natives Monterey pine and Monterey cypress. Ironically, of the three species, the blue gum is the only one that reproduces on its own in the park, since both native species require either fire or very hot prolonged summer heat (neither of which is common in San Francisco!) for their seeds to open.

California has not been entirely on the receiving end of botanical exchange with Oceania, however. One of the most important timber trees in Australia and New Zealand is California's Monterey pine *(Pinus radiata)*, which is known down under as "radiata pine." Monterey pine represents over 90 percent of the planted forest in New Zealand, where it is prized for its rapid growth and suitability for many uses.

JACARANDA

This warmth–loving tree is better known in Southern California, where it thrives. In San Francisco, jacarandas are hardy only in the city's sunniest and warmest microclimates (such as the Potrero Hill and Mission neighborhoods); they are rarely found in the western half of the city. The tree is easily recognized for its blossoms—showy, lavender, 2-inch tubular flowers that bloom in large clusters in late May through July. Jacarandas grow moderately quickly to 25–35 feet and have an open, oval-shaped canopy. This semievergreen tree has lacy, finely cut leaves that typically drop in late winter. Jacarandas are native to Brazil.

LOCATION: 618 Carolina St./19th St. on Potrero Hill; also at 3970 20th St./Sanchez St. in the Upper Market neighborhood

BLACK WALNUT

To be honest, you will not find many black walnuts in San Francisco, but here is what earns the tree a spot in this book: the sunlight sparkling through the canopy of this tree is an incredible sight if you are lying on the grass below and gazing upward. This high-branched tree can reach 125 feet in the wild, but as a city tree it is more likely to grow 50–75 feet in height. The tree produces small, edible nuts used in baking and as flavoring for ice cream. Native Americans, including the Cherokees and Iroquois, used the nuts in soups, breads, and puddings. The seeds are dispersed in the wild by squirrels, which bury them at a distance from the tree. Leaves are compound, with eleven to twenty-three leaflets. Black walnut is one of the most valuable

LOCATION: across from 1809 Oak St./Clayton St. in the Golden Gate Park panhandle

woods in the world, highly prized for furniture and as the favored wood for rifles and shotguns. As a result, many of the largest trees and best stands in its native range have been wiped out. Black walnut is native to a wide swath of the eastern United States, from Minnesota to Massachusetts, south to northern Florida and eastern Texas.

GRECIAN LAUREL; SWEET BAY

LOCATION: 555 Battery St./Jackson St. in the Financial District, in front of the U.S. Customs House; also at 206 Edgewood Ave. in Parnassus Heights

This is the classic laurel of antiquity—the symbol of victory and honor. The Greek word for laurel is *dhafni*, after the nymph Daphne in Greek mythology. According to the myth, the gods helped Daphne escape Apollo's attempted rape by turning her into a laurel tree. Apollo made the tree sacred, and it became a symbol of honor. The Greeks also began the tradition of crowning victors and distinguished persons with a wreath of laurel, from which we get the term "laureate." Since the Middle Ages, superstitions have credited laurel or bay with protective powers against witches, lightning, and even death.

This is also the traditional bay leaf used in cooking—not to be confused with the California bay (*Umbellularia californica*), which is native to the Bay Area but is much stronger as an herb. A native of the Mediterranean region, *Laurus nobilis* is a good San Francisco street tree, tolerating well our own Mediterranean conditions (dry summers, wind, fog, sandy soil). It is a handsome tree, resembling a ficus, with attractive, smooth gray bark and a dense evergreen canopy with dark glossy leaves. The small yellow flowers bloom in February and March and are followed by dark purple berries in female trees. The tree grows slowly to a height of 40–50 feet; the roots of mature trees can do significant damage to sidewalks.

AUSTRALIAN TEA TREE

LOCATION: 1278 Alemany Blvd./Silver Ave. in the Outer Mission; others nearby at 1249 and 1277 Alemany

is by nature a shrub, native to the coastal dunes of southeastern Australia and Tasmania. Because it tolerates sandy soils and windy conditions, the tree is an excellent windbreak near the ocean—it is used extensively on the western edge of Golden Gate Park. The foliage is an attractive gray-green, with oval leaves to 1 inch in length. Sprays of small white flowers bloom along stems and branches from April to June, followed by ¼-inch woody seed capsules that form during the summer and persist year-round.

The most interesting feature of this tree is its "muscular-looking, twisted and gracefully curved, shaggy, gray-brown trunk," as Sunset's *Western Garden Book* so aptly describes it. Although trainable as a tree, the Australian tea

Golden Gate Park and

STRYBING ARBORETUM

The first plans for an arboretum in Golden Gate Park were laid out by John McLaren, Golden Gate Park's superintendent for more than 50 years beginning in the 1880s. However, funding for the project had to wait until 1927, when Helene Strybing made a major bequest for an arboretum and botanical gardens "preferably in the vicinity of... the California Academy of Sciences," contain[ing] "plants ... properly labeled for purposes of information and instruction." Since then Strybing has grown into one of the leading arboretums in the United States. It is open to the public without charge every day of the year.

Although Strybing has a little of everything in its collection, I think the most impressive gardens are those highlighting trees and plants from the world's temperate and Mediterranean regions. Taking advantage of San Francisco's own Mediterranean climate, Strybing features separate gardens with collections from eastern Australia, western Australia, New Zealand, South Africa, and Chile, as well as a California native garden.

NEW ZEALAND TEA TREE

LOCATION: Plymouth St./Monterey Blvd. near St. Francis Wood; also at 2065 Vallejo St./Webster St. in Pacific Heights

Known as *manuka* in its native New Zealand, the name "tea tree" was given to *Leptospermum scoparium* by Captain Cook. Historians believe that in 1777, Cook and a group of New Zealand's native Maoris got together to drink a tea made from the tree's leaves. The leaves are an excellent source of vitamin C, which helped prevent scurvy, a common disease among sailors in the eighteenth century. (I recommend sticking to orange juice today—it is not a tasty tea.) Compounds from this tree are used as insecticides, and oils from the tree are used as perfumes in soap, toothpaste, and deodorant.

This small tree rarely grows taller than 15 feet and is easily recognizable by its showy flowers and needle–like leaves. Most common in San Francisco is the 'Ruby Glow' variety, which has reddish pink flowers that bloom profusely during the spring and summer. The 'Helene Strybing' variety, named after the benefactor of Strybing Arboretum, produces deep pink flowers.

GLOSSY PRIVET

LOCATION: Guerrero near 22nd St. in the Mission; also at 1355 Guerrero St./25th St. in the Mission

Most of the privet species are shrubs, frequently used as hedges; the glossy privet is the only species used as a street tree. The dark, evergreen, glossy foliage of this tree forms a round, dense canopy that can reach 20–30 feet. Creamy white flowers in the spring attract bees but sometimes repel humans (the earthy fragrance of privet flowers is an acquired taste). The clusters of flowers form a pyramid shape and are followed by small bluish berries. As mature trees, privets that are neglected will develop a dense outer canopy that gradually kills the interior growth, leaving unsightly dead branches. The tree is native to China, Korea, and Japan.

AMERICAN SWEETGUM

LOCATION: 2385 Bryant St./22nd St. in the Mission; many examples on Stanyan St. between 17th and Belgrave Sts. in Cole Valley

If, like me, you're from east of the Mississippi and associate trees with leafy maples, this is your Bay Area substitute. Although native to the humid southeastern United States, American sweetgum thrives in San Francisco's Mediterranean–type climate. Its medium green, distinctive maple–like leaves turn yellow, orange, and red in the fall, although the colors are not as brilliant in San Francisco as in warmer inland climates. It is considered a deciduous tree, but exactly when a particular tree loses its leaves depends on the specimen—in San Francisco, some trees retain their old leaves until the following spring, when new leaves arrive, sometimes as late as May or early June. Other specimens are leafless all winter—it just depends on the tree. American sweetgums have insignificant flowers, followed by round, spiny seed capsules in the winter. This is one of San Francisco's larger street trees, growing in an oval form to 40–50 feet in height. However, the limbs can be brittle in mature specimens, and regular pruning is recommended for older trees to reduce the risk of limb loss in winter storms (my neighborhood was littered with sweetgum limbs during a severe December 1995 windstorm). Pest and disease resistant, this is a great choice for a street tree if you don't mind some sidewalk damage from its invasive roots. With long, straight trunks, sweetgums are an important timber tree in the Southeast; the wood is used for furniture, cabinets, and veneers.

TULIP TREE

If a tree can be considered noble, the tulip tree is high in the ranks of arboreal gentry. It is one of the largest of North America's broadleaf trees, capable of growing to a stately 200 feet in ideal conditions. Mature trees have a long, clean trunk that rises high before branching out (the Native Americans of Pennsylvania and Virginia made dugout canoes from the trunks). Tulip trees are long lived, with average life spans of 200–250 years. No other tree has a leaf quite this shape—sometimes described as lyre shaped, it looks like a five-point maple leaf without the top lobe. Trees 15–20 years old develop large, handsome, tulip–like flowers that are greenish yellow, with a deep orange band at the center. However, because of the height of the tree by that time, binoculars to see the flowers are needed. In their native habitat, tulip trees range from southern New England west to Michigan and south to northern Florida and Louisiana. They are most abundant and reach their largest size in the Ohio River Valley and on the slopes of the Appalachians (the tulip tree is the state tree of Indiana, Kentucky, and Tennessee).

LOCATION: Sansome Street between Sacramento and Commercial Sts. in front of the old Federal Reserve building in the Financial District. Many large tulip trees also line University Ave. in Berkeley.

BRISBANE BOX

LOCATION: 333 Franklin St./Grove St. in the Civic Center area—this relatively young tree already demonstrates the Brisbane box's upright form. Also at 696 2nd Ave./Cabrillo St. in the Richmond; 1634 Fell St./Masonic Ave. in the Haight-Ashbury. Many examples on Gough and Franklin Sts. between Market and Grove Sts. in the Civic Center area.

In recent years the Brisbane box has become one of the most commonly planted large trees in San Francisco. It has a lot to like: attractive, dark evergreen foliage in a distinctive "tree-like," upright oval form; smooth, reddish brown peeling bark reminiscent of California's madrone trees; resistance to pests and diseases; and tolerance of wind, fog, dry summers, sidewalks, and poor soil. In addition, the tree needs very low maintenance; it produces no significant leaf or flower drop, and for a large tree (it can easily reach 40 feet), it is relatively kind to sidewalks. Some people find this tree a bit dull, because its white flowers are nothing to write home about when they bloom in July and August and have no olfactory charm.

Dull it may be, but reliability counts for something in San Francisco's harsh (for trees) urban environment, which explains the Brisbane box's increasing popularity on the city streets (it is the sixth most frequently planted tree in San Francisco). It is so common in San Francisco's Tenderloin neighborhood that some locals refer to it as the "Tenderloin tree." Native to the forests of eastern Australia, the Brisbane box is also one of the most common street trees in Sydney, Melbourne, and other cities down under.

CATALINA IRONWOOD

LOCATION: northeast corner of Connecticut and 19th Sts. on Potrero Hill; also on Hermann St. near Market St. in the Upper Market area

The Catalina ironwood is one of the few California native trees planted on San Francisco streets. Although fossil records prove that this tree was once widespread throughout California, it is now limited in the wild to the Channel Islands of Santa Catalina, Santa Cruz, Santa Rosa, and San Clemente off the Southern California coast. The sub-species *asplenifolius* (the type seen in San Francisco) is found only on Santa Catalina. This tree demonstrates how islands often develop unique flora as environmental threats from the main-land (in this case, perhaps plant–eating animals) are stopped at water's edge.

Catalina ironwood was first discovered in 1884 by William Lyon and named in his honor, but it was pioneering nurseryman Francisco Franceschi who introduced this tree into the nursery trade. Upon finding that the tree was difficult to germinate from seed or branch cuttings, he set out to the Channel Islands to collect a full-grown specimen with large enough roots to permit root cuttings. Suspected as an outlaw by the Coast Guard, he was fired upon until his vessel began to leak. Furiously bailing water, he managed to reach Santa Barbara Harbor with his prize in hand. Young plants from this specimen were introduced to nurseries a few years later.

Ironically, today this plant is used and appreciated all over the world but is threatened in its native habitat of the Channel Islands as a result of grazing by introduced feral goats.

In addition to its interesting history, this tree has a distinctive appearance. The *asplenifolius* subspecies (the type most often planted as an ornamental) has deep green, glossy leaves divided into three to seven leaflets. Each leaflet is deeply notched, giving a fernlike grace to the entire tree. The bark is reddish brown and peels into narrow vertical strips. In May and June, the tree becomes covered with small white blossoms that occur in large flat clusters 3–6 inches wide.

A Catalina ironwood in full bloom.

The Controversy About

NATIVE PLANTS

If one "tree issue" has captured San Francisco's attention in recent years, it is the native plant controversy. This well-matched fight pits two earnest and passionate groups against one another: the native plant enthusiasts, trying to preserve what is left of San Francisco's dwindling natural environment, and the tree lovers—whose affection extends to all trees, including "immigrants" like the eucalyptus.

San Francisco's Natural Areas Program is a division of the Recreation and Parks Department, charged with preserving native plants and restoring native habitats. During the course of their restoration work, the Natural Areas Program gardeners have removed a number of mature nonnative trees in areas such as McLaren Park, Mount Davidson, Bayview Hill, and Tank Hill overlooking Cole Valley. The primary victim: the blue gum eucalyptus (*Eucalyptus globulus*), which the Natural Areas Program claims "has few natural predators, rapid growth rates, and shades and poisons nearby sun-loving natives by exuding [its] own natural herbicides."

The native plant enthusiasts have a point. Eucalyptus do have a way of taking over, elbowing out other species until a single-species "monoculture" is created. Have you ever tried to walk through a mature eucalyptus forest that has been left to its own for a while (for example, Sutro Forest)? Underneath the canopy, you'll find an impenetrable tangle of blackberry thorns and ivy. Creating some areas where native oaks, willows, and buckeyes can thrive in an ecosystem with other native plants does not seem so extreme.

On the other hand, without introduced trees, San Francisco would be a pretty dreary place. Virtually all of San Francisco's street trees are nonnative, since native trees are usually poor choices for street plantings (they either grow too large or do not tolerate being planted in sidewalks). And for many settings, there is nothing better than a big, majestic, aromatic eucalyptus—I could not imagine California without the sight and smell of this Australian import.

So stay tuned as the supporters and opponents of the Natural Areas Program battle it out. And let's hope both groups get at least some of what they want.

SOUTHERN MAGNOLIA

LOCATION: west side of 18th St. in Dolores Park, near Church St. Many large specimens border this park on 18th and 20th Sts.

This evergreen tree is native to the southern United States, from North Carolina to central Florida and west to eastern Texas. Southern magnolia's popularity has made it an icon of southern grace and charm; in fact, its flower is the state flower of Mississippi and Louisiana. In California, the tree will reach heights of 25–45 feet, depending on the variety, with leaves that are waxy and glossy green above and often rust colored beneath. Large, showy, and very fragrant white flowers (8–10 inches across) bloom from March to July, followed by conical seed capsules that look like small hand grenades. Magnolias do not always thrive in our urban conditions

and dry, Mediterranean climate, but they are popular enough to be in the top 10 (at #9) of most frequently planted San Francisco trees.

The magnolia family is one of the most primitive groups of flowering plants (angiosperms) in evolutionary history, having emerged at a time when the only plants on earth were conifers and ferns. The magnolia's primitive mystique is enhanced by its unchanged method of pollination—by beetles. (Magnolias predate the evolution of bees and butterflies, which are more traditional pollinators.)

Fossil records suggest that magnolias were found throughout the Northern Hemisphere before the Ice Age. As the earth's climate cooled and the glaciers advanced, the species was forced southward. In Europe, the tree's southward retreat was blocked by the Alps and the Mediterranean Sea, causing the loss of the European species.

MAYTEN

The mayten is a favorite of many San Francisco tree lovers for its graceful, weeping form. This evergreen grows slowly to 25–30 feet, with long, pendulous branchlets reminiscent of weeping willows (although the two trees are not closely related). The mayten's narrow, bright green leaves are 1–2 inches long, and both the flowers and fruit are inconspicuous. Maytens are native to Chile. The species name *boaria* means "relating to cattle" and refers to the fondness grazing cattle have for the foliage of this tree in South America. San Franciscans' fondness for the mayten has helped to push it to the #8 spot among the city's most frequently planted street trees.

LOCATION: across from 1685 Oak St./Ashbury St. in the Golden Gate Park panhandle; also at 1248 5th Ave./Hugo St. in the Sunset

LOCATION: Albion Street between 16th and 17th Sts. in the Mission, which is also the site of the first Spanish encampment in San Francisco in 1776. Also on the 200 block of Texas St./Mariposa St. on Potrero Hill.

The *Melaleuca* genus is big, with over 200 species in the plants' native Australia, Indonesia, and New Guinea. Most melaleucas share a few common characteristics: small narrow or needle-like evergreen leaves, spongy or papery whitish bark that peels off in layers, and a rapid growth rate. *Melaleuca linarifolia* is the most common melaleuca in San Francisco and has all these features: the 1-inch leaves are indeed needle-like, resembling those of some conifers; the whitish bark sheds in papery flakes; and the tree grows rapidly to 25 feet. What distinguishes this tree, and why is it San Francisco's favorite melaleuca? I think it is the flowers. In June, flaxleaf paperbarks bloom with spikes of fluffy, bottlebrush-like flowers; the small white blossoms are so dense that the trees resemble giant cotton balls or snow—the tree's common name in its native Australia is "snow in summer."

CAJEPUT TREE

Of the 200+ varieties of *Melaleuca* in Australia, the cajeput is the one most commonly cultivated; Australian sources refer to it as the "quintessential" melaleuca. Called "broad-leafed paperbark" down under, this tree has gray-green, leathery, 2–4-inch oval leaves and grows quickly to 20–30 feet. The tree's spongy white bark can be easily peeled off in sheets and is used as a lining for hanging baskets. The yellowish white flowers bloom in clusters from June to August, but they are not as showy as those of the flaxleaf paperbark. The cup-shaped 3/16-inch seed capsules form in clusters 2–3 inches long, and they can persist on branches for a year or longer. Cajeputs are well adapted to San Francisco's conditions, tolerating poor and even salty soil and strong winds.

LOCATION: 4438–4444 18th St./Douglass St. in the Castro; also at Bryant St. near 18th St. in the Mission

The cajeput is a serious environmental threat to the Everglades and southern Florida, where it is growing explosively, turning the natural grassy wetlands into dense melaleuca thickets. The tree was introduced into southern Florida in the early 1900s for "swamp drying." Having no natural enemies, it began to spread aggressively, crowding out the native vegetation that is essential for supporting animal life. Biological control may offer some hope, however. The U.S. Department of Agriculture is releasing several species of Australian snout beetles, which are specific to melaleuca and feed on its shoots, reducing the plant's ability to reproduce.

NEW ZEALAND CHRISTMAS TREE

LOCATION: a rare yellow 'Aurea' variety at 1221 Stanyan St./17th St. in Cole Valley; many examples line Roosevelt Way in the Upper Market area

In its native New Zealand, this ever-green is known as *pohutukawa*—an aboriginal Maori word that means "drenched with spray." That definition aptly describes the seashore conditions in which these trees grow in coastal New Zealand, and it also explains why the tree is so well adapted to San Francisco's coastal conditions. The tree's showy red bottlebrush–like flowers peak from late May to early July—the flowers bloom at Christmastime in New Zealand, creating a green–and–red effect that gives the tree its common name. The flowers are followed by ¼ -inch seed capsules. The oval leaves are an attractive gray-green. Another distinguishing feature of the tree is its aerial root system, an adaptation that helps the tree search for crevices and pockets of soil on the rocky cliffs of coastal New Zealand.

New Zealand Christmas tree is one of San Francisco's most common trees—it is #3 in popularity according to the past 20 years' planting records. It grows moderately fast to 30 feet or more and is extremely well adapted to San Francisco's climate—of all the city's trees, it is the most tolerant of wind, fog, and poor soil. This is an excellent choice for neighborhoods near the ocean, where sandy soil, wind, fog, and salt air prove inhospitable for other species. The downside: the tree's aggressive roots are among the worst sidewalk breakers of any San Francisco street tree.

The rare 'Aurea' variety of this tree, with yellow flowers, was derived from two trees discovered on Motiti Island in New Zealand's Bay of Plenty in 1940.

The (normally) red flowers and green foliage of the New Zealand Christmas tree.

MYOPORUM

invasive roots, an unruly growth pattern (it grows in a dense mass in every direction, making pruning difficult), and very poisonous leaves. Myoporums were planted heavily as an experimental street tree in the 1960s and 1970s. They are no longer permitted to be planted as street trees in San Francisco, but you'll see a lot of older, mature specimens breaking sidewalks in the city's neighborhoods.

LOCATION: corner of Geary and Masonic Sts.; a row of trees stands on Central Ave. between Page and Oak Sts. in the Haight-Ashbury

This hardy, fast-growing tree is superbly adapted to San Francisco's cool, windy, and foggy coastal climate, which is why it is densely planted on the western border of Golden Gate Park to block the wind and blowing sand. Unfortunately, the myoporum is a bad choice as a street tree. It has

Myoporum is native to New Zealand, where it is known by the Maori name *ngaio*. The bright green leaves have translucent pores that are easily visible if held up to sunlight—the tree's name is from the Greek *poros* (pores).

OLIVE

LOCATION: 200 block of Carolina St./Mariposa St. on Potrero Hill, in Jackson St. playground; also at 1830 Lyon St./Sacramento St. in Pacific Heights (many examples on Sacramento St. from Lyon to Divisadero Sts.); Hyde St. on either side of Bay St. at the base of Russian Hill

"The olive tree is the richest gift of heaven," wrote Thomas Jefferson. I might vote for a McIntosh apple tree, myself, but he had a point—the olive tree for centuries has represented humankind's domestication of plants:

food from its fruit; light from its oil; symbols of peace from its branches! Evidence of olive stones from archaeological sites in the eastern Mediterranean suggests that olives have been consumed since about 9000 B.C., although only from 3500 B.C. is there evidence of domestication (on the island of Crete). Olives were among the first trees to be introduced to California by Europeans, in the mid–1700s by early Spanish missionaries.

Olive trees grow slowly to 30 feet, and they can be exceptionally graceful and beautiful, particularly if well pruned. An evergreen, the tree has narrow, gray–green leaves, a smooth gray trunk, and branches that can become beautifully gnarled with age. Olive trees can last a long, long time—if cared for properly, olives can live hundreds of years (olive trees in the garden of Gethsemene in Israel are said to date back 2,000 years, although that result will never happen on a San Francisco street). Olives love the sun and can tolerate drought and poor soils, as they do in their native, rocky Greece.

AVOCADO

The avocado is native to the Americas—it is widely distributed throughout Central and South America, ranging from eastern Mexico through Central America to the northern Andes. Human beings have appreciated the avocado for thousands of years. Avocado seeds dating to 7000 B.C. have been found at Mexican archaeological sites, and experts believe that the Aztecs cultivated the plant as early as 500 B.C. The experts know this because the pits in more recent archaeological deposits are larger, suggesting that natives were cultivating plants from seeds selected on the basis of fruit size. The Aztecs had an interesting anthropomorphic association with this tree—the common Spanish name for the tree is *aguacate,* from the Aztec *ahuacatl,* meaning "tree with testicles."

Conquistador Hernán Cortés discovered the avocado in 1519 when he was the first European to arrive in Mexico City. A few years later, the Spanish historian Oviedo wrote the first description of the avocado: "In the center of the fruit is a seed like a peeled chestnut. And between this and the rind is the part which is eaten, which is abundant, and is a paste similar to butter and of very good taste."

LOCATION: 1011 South Van Ness Ave./21st St. in the Mission; also at 438 Arkansas St. on Potrero Hill

The Spanish soon introduced the avocado to the West Indies, the Canary Islands, and other possessions around the world.

Avocados were introduced to Florida in the 1830s, but not until the twentieth century did the avocado industry really take off in the United States, in California. Carl Schmidt, a 21-year-old employee of a nursery in Altadena, California, was sent to Mexico in 1911 to search for the country's best avocados and bring back cuttings of the trees from which they came. On his return, many cuttings refused to adapt to California's soil and cooler climate, but one flourished; when it survived the great freeze of 1913, it was given the name *fuerte*, the Spanish word for "strong." This tree is credited with starting California's avocado industry. The famous 'Hass' variety originated in 1935 when Rudolph Hass, a postman and amateur farmer in La Habra, California, discovered a superior tree in his 2-acre orchard (the tree can still be seen in La Habra).

Avocado flowers are cross-pollinated, meaning that flowers of one tree can be pollinated only by pollen from another tree—a botanical trick that encourages genetic diversity. Cross-pollination is actually achieved by the stigma (the female part of the flower) becoming receptive to male flowers' pollen before the pollen is released from flowers of the same tree. (This is one reason why avocado trees rarely set fruit in San Francisco—not enough other avocados are nearby!) The large seed of the avocado is an adaptation for supplying young plants with enough food to enable them to survive in the dark forest undergrowth until they can attract enough light to survive.

It is unfortunate that avocado trees are not more common on San Francisco streets, because almost all the specimens that can be found around the city are beautiful and healthy trees. Even if they do not produce much fruit in the city, avocado trees are attractive ornamentals, with handsome glossy foliage and an open branching pattern that easily reaches to 35 feet.

CANARY ISLAND PALM

LOCATION: The Embarcadero near Brannan St., with the Bay Bridge in the background. Canary Island palms line the Embarcadero from Fisherman's Wharf to Mission Bay, as well as upper Market St. from Octavia to Castro Sts.

Twenty years ago, I'm not sure I would have strongly associated palm trees and San Francisco. Los Angeles, sure, but San Francisco? Since the early 1990s, however, Canary Island palms have been used extensively in high-profile, major street landscaping projects in San Francisco. In 1993, the tree was used to line the entire length of upper Market St., to spectacular effect. In the late 1990s, Canary Island palms were used to landscape the city's waterfront along the Embar-cadero, from Mission Bay all the way to Fisherman's Wharf, replacing the elevated freeway that formerly cut off the city from its bay views. Plenty of San Franciscans complained at the time, concerned that the palms were "Los Angelizing" the city. Fortunately, they lost that aesthetic battle, and the stately Canary Island palm is now very much part of the San Francisco fabric.

The Canary Island palm supposedly was introduced to California by Spanish priests during the eighteenth century. The tree has a massive trunk—4–5 feet in diameter—which in its natural state is roughened by the woody remnants of old palm fronds. In cultivation, the trunk is usually trimmed to a smooth cylinder. The gracefully arching leaves are 15–20 feet long, with 2–inch–wide leaflets 12–16 inches long. Cream–colored flowers appear in clusters, with male and female flowers on different trees; the female trees produce (inedible) clusters of datelike ¾-inch seeds in the fall. The tree is native to Spain's Canary Islands, in the Atlantic off the southwest coast of Morocco.

ITALIAN STONE PINE

The Italian stone pine is the tree that produces the pine nuts used in Mediterranean cuisine. Of the 100+ pine species worldwide, it was the first pine used and cultivated by humans. The seeds have been harvested for an estimated 500,000 years, and the tree likely has been in cultivation for over 6,000 years. It is hard to know the original range of the Italian stone pine, since it was spread by human cultivation before historical records were kept. However, before human-induced range expansions, this tree was probably confined to the Iberian Peninsula, which is the only area where it is found away from ancient trade routes.

LOCATION: Corner of Fernwood Dr. and El Verano Way; also at 90 Woodland Ave. in Cole Valley; in median across from 410 Miramar Ave./Southwood Dr. in Westwood Park; many examples on Portola Dr. from Woodside Ave. to Claremont Blvd.

Italian stone pines are noted for their broad, umbrella-shaped crown. The reddish brown bark is distinctive—it is deeply fissured and comes off in thin plates. The tree's 5–7-inch-long, glossy green needles are held in bundles of two. (This is one of the best ways to identify particular pine species—the needles are arranged in bunches that range from two to five, but always the same number within a species.) The baseball-sized cones change color as they ripen, from green, through various shades of purple, to brown. The brown seeds are dispersed by birds (and, during the past 6,000 years, *Homo sapiens* have helped).

MONTEREY PINE

LOCATION: corner of Willard St. and Belmont Ave. in Parnassus Heights; also at 320 Magellan Ave./Dorantes Ave. in Forest Hill; median of 10th Ave. just north of Lake St. in the Richmond

When you fly over San Francisco and see the green of its parks, much of what you are viewing is the canopy of the Monterey pine, one of San Francisco's three most common park trees. Together, Monterey pine, Monterey cypress (*Cupressus macrocarpa*), and blue gum (*Eucalyptus globulus*) account for over 90 percent of the forest canopy in Golden Gate Park and most other San Francisco parks. Monterey pine is almost never seen as a street tree because of its size (it tops out at 100 feet) and its invasive, shallow roots.

Monterey pines are native to three small and completely separate areas on the central California coast: the northernmost near Año Nuevo State Park in Santa Cruz County; the largest covering the entire Monterey Peninsula; and the southernmost near San Luis Obispo. A related variety of Monterey pine is found on the islands of Guadalupe and Cedros off the coast of Baja California, Mexico. Despite its tiny natural range, Monterey pine is one of the most commonly planted trees in the world. It is used extensively in Southern Hemisphere timber plantations because of the excellent quality of its wood and its amazingly rapid growth rate (reputedly, some tree rings of Monterey pine are 1½ inches apart!). It is also the most widely grown softwood tree in Australia and New Zealand—which makes it a good trade for all the trees imported from down under and used as street trees here in California.

Monterey pines have an irregular, open canopy that can be very attractive as a specimen tree. The 3–6-inch needles are arranged in bundles of three (this is one of the easiest ways to tell one species of pine from another) and hang densely on the tree. The tree's egg-shaped 3–5-inch cones remain closed on the tree for several years at a time, opening during periods of very warm weather (in fact, fire is the best agent for seed propagation of Monterey pine).

Unfortunately, Monterey pine in California is under serious attack from pitch canker (*Fusarium subglutinans*), an often–fatal fungal disease native to the southeastern United States. The disease, believed to be transmitted by bark beetles from tree to tree, was discovered in California in 1986, and it reached San Francisco in 1992. In many areas 80 to 90 percent of the trees are affected. Presently no cure for pitch canker exists. However, genetic resistance appears to be present in at least some specimens of Monterey pine, offering hope for the long–term survival of the species. Efforts are being made to breed resistant trees, but until resistant varieties are available, Monterey pines are not being planted in San Francisco parks.

TREE DISEASES

in San Francisco

The turn of the twenty-first century has not been a good time for Bay Area trees. In 1986, pine pitch canker, a fungal disease long affecting pines from the southern United States, was first detected in California. The disease was first discovered in Santa Cruz, but is now found from San Diego to Mendocino County. Pitch canker is known to affect several varieties of California pines, but the Monterey pine *(Pinus radiata),* one of San Francisco's most important park and landscape trees, has been hardest hit. The disease is characterized first by the browning and dieback of branches, starting with the top of the tree, followed by the oozing of pitch (hence the name) from the branches and trunk, with death often the final result. Pitch canker is not always fatal, and some recent evidence indicates that trees infected in the 1980s are now developing resistance to the disease. However, this disease is a major disaster for San Francisco's parks and neighborhoods, and it will be years before the full impact of the disease is felt. One recent impact of pitch canker: there is now a moratorium on the planting of Monterey pines in the city's parks, meaning that our parks could have a very different look in the not too distant future.

An even worse disaster looms with a more recent disease. Sudden oak death is a disease that has killed large numbers of tanoaks *(Lithocarpus densiflorus),* coast live oaks *(Quercus agrifolia),* and black oaks *(Quercus kelloggii)* since its discovery on a tanoak in Mill Valley, California. The disease has since spread to the entire Bay Area. In 2000, University of California researchers isolated the pathogen: a new, fungus-like alga (similar to the disease that ravaged Ireland's potato crops in the 1840s) that they named *Phytophthora ramorum.* Recent research is even more alarming, suggesting that the disease can affect other native trees, such as California bay, madrone, buckeye, Douglas fir, and even redwood trees. Early signs of sudden oak death are bleeding cankers and leaf spots, often leading to the death of the tree. The alarming breadth of the potential hosts for this disease and the high mortality rate among some of the early species affected makes the disease a real threat. Imagine California without oaks, bay laurels, madrones, Douglas firs, and redwoods, and you'll appreciate the potential severity of the problem.

VICTORIAN BOX

LOCATION: 1403 Willard St./Parnassus Ave. in Cole Valley; also at 132 10th Ave./Lake St. in the Richmond

The perfume of this tree outdoes any other during its springtime blooming season—the fragrance (similar to orange blossoms) is so strong that I often know one is nearby without even seeing it! Partly because of its olfactory appeal, this evergreen tree is now #7 on the list of most frequently planted trees in San Francisco. It has attractive, dark green foliage with glossy, wavy-edged, narrow leaves, 3–6 inches long (the new foliage is brighter green, making an attractive two-tone color scheme during the spring growth spurt). Profuse clusters of creamy white, bell-shaped flowers emerge en masse in February, but trees often continue to bloom until May. They are followed by clusters of sticky, ½-inch orange fruits that can become a mess as they open and fall in late autumn and winter. Native to Australia, the Victorian box has become an invasive pest in many tropical countries, including the Caribbean and Polynesia. In the wild, it reproduces from seed with the help of birds, who eat the fruit and then excrete the seed. This is the largest of the many species of Pittosporum; its rounded crown can reach 40 feet or more.

LONDON PLANE TREE

LOCATION: near the corner of San Anselmo and San Buenaventura Sts. in St. Francis Wood. The tree has been pollarded; that is, repeatedly cut back to specific points on the tree to create bulbous knobs. Large London plane trees line Bryant St. between 6th and 7th Sts. in front of the Hall of Justice; California St. is lined with pollarded London planes for virtually its entire length.

The London plane tree is probably the most popular urban tree in the world—and one of the most beautiful, under the right conditions. It is a common tree in San Francisco, but it is the biggest arboreal mistake in the city. These trees are not happy in San Francisco's windy, foggy environment, and they often suffer from anthracnose and powdery mildew—fungal diseases that spot and disfigure leaves.

In ideal conditions, the London plane is striking. Reaching a height of 80 feet, the tree has attractive mottled bark and large, five-lobed leaves resembling those of maples. It is deciduous and has a beautiful winter silhouette, with ball-shaped fruit clusters that hang on the tree, often until spring. In other parts of the world, the London plane has adapted well to difficult urban conditions, and human beings have responded by planting it almost to the point of monocultural excess—an estimated 60 percent of London's trees are London planes, and Paris is not far behind. San Francisco urban planners may have had similar images in mind when they decided to line Market St., our "main street," with London planes. Unfortunately, like most London planes in San Francisco, the Market St. trees are a disappointment.

The *Platanus* x *acerifolia* hybrid was born in London in the 1660s, the product of crossing oriental planes (*Platanus orientalis*) from southeastern Europe and Asia Minor with American sycamores (*Platanus occidentalis*), which English plant breeders had recently introduced from the New World. London planes are often pollarded—a pruning method in which all the tree's growth is removed annually. New branches can emerge wherever cuts are made.

LOMBARDY POPLAR

LOCATION: near the corner of Clay and Drumm Sts.; Embarcadero Center in the background. The Lombardy poplars in this park are the nightly home of San Francisco's wild parrots.

This easily recognizable tree is known for its strongly vertical form—the tree can easily reach 70–80 feet in height, but it is rarely more than 10–15 feet wide. Lombardy poplars do not make great street trees, because their inva-

sive roots break sidewalks and attack underground utilities. In rural areas, these trees are frequently used as windbreaks or to line country driveways. In San Francisco, this tree was often planted in rows alongside elevated freeways (such as the former Embarcadero and Central freeways) to screen them from nearby city neighborhoods. Now that many of these freeways have come down, the remaining rows of trees serve as a reminder of the past—since they still outline the former route. (You can trace the former Washington Street exits to the Embarcadero freeway in the park near Embarcadero Three in the Financial District.) Lombardy poplar has 2–4-inch triangular leaves that emerge in late April/early May after the male catkins (flowers) have released their pollen; these deciduous trees lose their leaves in the fall. This tree is believed to have emerged as a variety of black poplar during the late 1600s in the Lombardy region of Italy. Lombardy poplar grows quickly, and like many fast-growing trees, has a short life span (rarely more than 40 years).

Prunus cerasifera

PURPLE-LEAF PLUM

LOCATION: 4958 17th St./Stanyan St. in Cole Valley; also at 2709 21st St./York St. in the Mission; 101 Woodland Ave./Willard St. in Parnassus Heights. The Parnassus Heights neighborhood is densely planted with plum trees and becomes a tourist attraction at peak bloom in late January/February.

This is the most popular tree in San Francisco—ranked #1 in Friends of the Urban Forest's planting records over the past 20 years. It is too popular for the tastes of some tree connoisseurs, who view it as an overplanted and unimaginative choice. In my neighborhood of Parnassus Heights, purple-leaf plum is the dominant street tree, and I have one planted in front of my own house. The tree is popular nationwide as well—over fifty cultivars and hybrids of this tree exist. Purple-leaf plums are one of the first of the flowering trees to bloom, producing showy light pink flowers in late January or February. The eponymous purple leaves emerge shortly after the flowers fade. The tree does not often grow past 25 feet, so it is a good choice under utility wires. Downside: in San Francisco the trees begins to lose their leaves in August, and many trees are bare by September. The tree does not tolerate wind well, so is not a good choice for the city's windy east–west streets. The wild form of this tree (native to southeastern Europe and central Asia) has green leaves and white flowers, but it is rare as a street tree. The purple–leaf cultivar is often grafted onto the wild, green–leafed variety, which is why you often see green–leafed sprouts pushing up from the rootstock.

SAN FRANCISCO'S TOP 20

Which trees are San Francisco's most popular? Since 1981 Friends of the Urban Forest has kept data on the 35,000 trees San Franciscans planted through its program. The data offers an interesting peek into the city's most popular trees, ranked by number of trees planted.

	TREE	ORIGIN
1	purple-leaf plum (*Prunus cerasifera*)	Cultivation
2	Japanese flowering cherry (*Prunus serrulata*)	Japan
3	New Zealand Christmas tree (*Metrosideros excelsus*)	New Zealand
4	small-leaf tristania (*Tristaniopsis laurina*)	Australia
5	strawberry tree (*Arbutus unedo*)	Europe
6	Brisbane box (*Lophostemon confertus*)	Australia
7	Victorian box (*Pittosporum undulatum*)	Australia
8	mayten (*Maytenus boaria*)	South America
9	southern magnolia (*Magnolia grandiflora*)	United States
10	ficus (*Ficus microcarpa*)	Asia
11	Bailey's acacia (*Acacia baileyana*)	Australia
12	bronze loquat (*Eriobotrya deflexa*)	Asia
13	Indian hawthorn (*Rhaphiolepsis* 'Majestic Beauty')	Asia
14	hopseed (*Dodonaea viscosa*)	Australia; others
15	cajeput tree (*Melaleuca quinquenervia*)	Australia
16	callery pear (*Pyrus calleryana*)	Asia
17	ginkgo (*Ginkgo biloba*)	Asia
18	olive (*Olea europaea*)	Mediterranean
19	glossy privet (*Ligustrum lucidum*)	Asia
20	evergreen pear (*Pyrus kawakamii*)	Taiwan

Of the top 20 trees, not one is a California native, and only the magnolia is native to the United States. But 7 of the 20 hail from Australia or New Zealand. These rankings would have looked different 20 years ago, as once-popular trees have fallen out of favor. The ficus is the best example—formerly San Francisco's most common street tree, arborists realized its limitations when many of the trees died during a freak 1991 winter freeze.

MELBOURNE'S TOP 20

Since so many of San Francisco's trees are from Australia, let's compare San Francisco's top 20 to the top 20 trees of Melbourne, a city at about the same latitude south of the equator as San Francisco is north. Here is the list—it appears that Melbourne is even more attached to Australian trees than we are, with 14 of the top 20 trees from Australia. Interestingly, Melbourne's list has two trees native to the United States—twice as many as on the San Francisco list.

	TREE	ORIGIN
1	Brisbane box *(Lophostemon confertus)*	Australia
2	flaxleaf paperbark *(Melaleuca linarifolia)*	Australia
3	purple-leaf plum *(Prunus cerasifera)*	Cultivation
4	prickly melaleuca *(Melaleuca styphelioides)*	Australia
5	London plane tree *(Platanus x acerifolia)*	Hybrid
6	white bottlebrush *(Callistemon salignus)*	Australia
7	eucalyptus *(various species)*	Australia
8	pin oak *(Quercus palustris)*	United States
9	lemon bottlebrush *(Callistemon citrinus)*	Australia
10	red flowering gum *(Corymbia ficifolia)*	Australia
11	peppermint willow *(Agonis flexuosa)*	Australia
12	flowering plum *(Prunus x blireiana)*	Hybrid
13	white ironbark *(Eucalyptus leucoxylon)*	Australia
14	weeping bottlebrush *(Callistemon viminalis)*	Australia
15	drooping melaleuca *(Melaleuca armillaris)*	Australia
16	Japanese flowering cherry *(Prunus serrulata)*	Japan
17	cow itch tree *(Lagunaria patersonii)*	Australia
18	American sweetgum *(Liquidambar styraciflua)*	United States
19	Nichol's willow-leafed peppermint tree *(Eucalyptus nicholii)*	Asia
20	lilly-pilly tree *(Acmena smithii)*	Australia

SOURCE: R. Beer, S. Frank, G. Waters, *Overview of Street Tree Populations in Melbourne—Turn of the 21st Century,* Institute of Land and Food Resources, University of Melbourne (2001).

JAPANESE FLOWERING CHERRY

San Franciscans love their flowering trees, and the flowering cherry is the city's #2 most frequently planted tree—right behind its close relative, the purple-leaf plum. There are more than 100 different cultivars of this popular tree, and 'Kwanzan' is by far the most common in San Francisco. In early April, this cultivar blooms with showy pink "double" flowers (that is, flowers with multiple layers of petals, looking something like a pom-pom) in large clumps along the stem. The 'Kwanzan' cultivar is sterile, so it produces no fruit. The leaves are medium green, oval, serrated, and 2–5 inches long, and they turn orange–yellow in autumn—this is one of the few trees to produce fall color in San Francisco. The tree is bare December to March.

The bark is also distinctive: thin, smooth, and reddish brown, with prominent horizontal lenticels. The tree can reach 15–25 feet in height, usually with a vase-shaped, spreading crown. Like most flowering cherries, *Prunus serrulata* is almost always grafted onto other varieties of cherry that have better resistance to root diseases. You can easily see where the graft occurred, because the diameter of the trunk typically shrinks sharply at this point, with the first branches spreading out just above the graft. *Prunus serrulata* is native to China, Japan, and Korea. Most of the cultivars have been developed in Japan, where the tree is a national symbol.

LOCATION: 1008–1010 Noe St./23rd St. in Noe Valley; also at 800 Junipero Serra Blvd./Lyndhurst Dr. in the Lakeside neighborhood

CALLERY PEAR

LOCATION: Mission Street between 3rd and 4th Streets in front of Yerba Buena gardens; also at 436 Cole St./Fell St. in the Haight-Ashbury

Two cultivars of callery pear are common on San Francisco streets. 'Aristocrat' is most common and has a rounded form. 'Chanticleer' has a more upright form. Each variety has dark green, glossy leaves that in hotter climates turn showy reds and scarlets in the fall, but only greens and yellows in cool, foggy San Francisco. The tree is bare from November to March, although individual trees can differ significantly in this aspect. Flowers appear in March, but in San Francisco this tree is not planted for its flowers, because it does not bloom well in the city's mild climate. Flowers are often followed by a few inconspicuous clusters of round, pea-sized, green or brown pears hidden amid the foliage. This fast-growing tree (particularly the 'Aristocrat' cultivar) reaches heights of 25–35 feet. Callery pear is native to China.

EVERGREEN PEAR

LOCATION: 101–105 Scott St./Waller St. in the lower Haight-Ashbury; also at 1299 18th St./ Texas St. on Potrero Hill

Evergreen pears are distinguished by a graceful, angular, branching pattern and a charcoal gray bark that with age develops an attractive cracked surface. Leaves are glossy, oval, and 2–4 inches long. The tree is deciduous in areas with harsh winters, but in San Francisco's mild climate, the leaves last until December or January, at which time they drop all at once (so count on some cleanup) and the new season's light green foliage emerges. The tree often develops leaf spot (dark brown or black spots on leaves) in San Francisco, particularly in foggier neighborhoods— it prefers the warmer and sunnier eastern side of town. Evergreen pears have white blooms in February and March, but like the callery pear, they do not bloom much in cool, foggy San Francisco. These are great trees under utility wires, as they rarely exceed 20–25 feet in height. The tree is native to Taiwan.

The distinctive, cracked, charcoal-colored bark of the evergreen pear.

CORK OAK

LOCATION: 4736 17th St./Cole St. in San Francisco—one of only two or three examples of this species on San Francisco's streets

This native of the western Mediterranean is the tree from which natural cork is made—the species name *suber* is Latin for "cork." The tree's bark is its distinctive feature; if you stick your finger into the fissures on the trunk of a cork oak, you'll be able to feel the spongy new bark from which cork is made. Cork is formed from multiple layers of strong cell walls that are both airtight and waterproof. This kind of bark protects the tree from two common environmental threats in the Mediterranean region: drought (watertight bark keeps moisture in) and fire (airtight bark acts as a fire retardant, preventing damage to the living layers inside and allowing the tree to rebound quickly even after severe fires).

According to records, cork was first used as a stopper for containers by the Egyptians, thousands of years ago. The ancient Greeks and Romans used cork oak bark in fishing buoys, sandals, beehives, home roofs, and ship construction, among other applications. The current use of cork as a stopper for wine bottles began during the late 1600s and is usually attributed to the French monk Dom Perignon, who is also credited with the creation of champagne. Although synthetic materials have replaced natural cork for many uses, the cork harvest continues today in Portugal, Spain, and other Mediterranean countries. In the commercial cork industry, the trunk and lower branches of the trees are entirely stripped of the outer layer of bark at 9-year intervals; care is taken to not damage the interior cork-producing cambium layer.

Cork oaks can grow 60 feet or higher, and can live 300–400 years under the right conditions. The oval leaves are shiny dark green above and grayish beneath. It is a shame that more cork oaks are not grown in San Francisco, because the few that exist as street trees are very successful.

ITALIAN BUCKTHORN

LOCATION: 343 Coleridge St./Cortland Ave. in Bernal Heights; also at 1245 Howard St./9th St. in South of Market

The reason to plant this tree is its foliage: dense, shiny, dark green leaves that are the image of health, on distinctive spear-like branches. The leaves are oval, to 2 inches long, and the flowers are small, pale green, and not showy. Flowers are followed by small black berries (on female trees only; the berries are both messy and poisonous, so it is rare to see a female tree on the streets). Although poisonous to humans, the berries are attractive to birds, which help to propagate the seeds in the wild through their droppings. Italian buckthorns are shrubs in their native southern Europe, but they can be trained as trees by pruning away side branches to create a central leader. The tree can grow 20–30 feet tall and 20 feet wide. Italian buckthorn has naturalized and become a pest in parts of Australia and New Zealand.

CALIFORNIA PEPPER TREE

LOCATION: 4019 26th St./Sanchez St. in Noe Valley; several examples on the east side of Castro St. between 21st and Liberty Sts. in the Castro

A mature California pepper arching over a backyard patio is a cliché of *Sunset* magazine's California lifestyle. Cliché or not, the California pepper is one of the most beautiful trees available to San Francisco tree lovers. Mature trees have wonderfully gnarled trunks, supporting rounded crowns of graceful, arching branches. The fernlike foliage is finely textured, with bright green leaves composed of many leaflets. California peppers have either male or female flowers; female flowers develop into drooping clusters of showy rose–colored peppercorn berries in the fall and winter. The seeds are sometimes sold as pink peppercorns, although in large quantities they can be toxic. (To avoid messy fruit drop, many city dwellers plant trees with male flowers only.) Like its relative the Brazilian pepper, this tree is related botanically to mangos, pistachios, and cashews, as well as to poison ivy and poison oak; contact with its leaves can cause dermatitis or allergic reactions in some individuals. Despite its common name, this tree is native not to California but to the Andes Mountains in Peru. It has, however, become naturalized in chaparral areas of Southern California.

BRAZILIAN PEPPER

The Brazilian pepper is a fast-growing, vigorous evergreen tree that is well adapted to city conditions. It has glossy, dark green compound leaves composed of five to thirteen leaflets, forming a rounded crown resembling that of a carob tree. The female trees (rarely planted on city streets) produce clusters of red berries, which are popular for use in Christmas wreaths. A shrub by nature, this tree does not develop a single straight trunk unless trained to do so—many examples of "crazy straw" Brazilian peppers are found where the trees have enjoyed only intermittent attention. Like many fast-growing trees, Brazilian peppers have brittle wood, so they need to have their canopies thinned to reduce risk of breakage in winter storms. Native to Brazil, the Brazilian pepper has become an invasive pest in Hawaii and Florida—in southern Florida it covers some 700,000 acres and is a severe threat to the native ecosystem.

LOCATION: 350 Santa Ana Ave./Ocean Ave. in St. Francis Wood; also many examples on Cabrillo St. between Arguello Blvd. and 3rd Ave. in the Richmond

COAST REDWOOD

LOCATION: Redwood Park, east side of the Transamerica Pyramid in the financial district; also across from 185 Castenada/Pacheco in Forest Hill. Muir Woods in Marin County is the best spot nearby to see coast redwoods in their native glory.

The coast redwood is the tallest tree on Earth, growing easily to more than 300 feet. (The tallest individual tree on Earth—measured at 367 feet in 1999—is a coast redwood in Montgomery Woods State Reserve near Ukiah, California.) These evergreen conifers are densely branched and gracefully pyramidal in shape, with flat, feathery needles and reddish brown, fibrous bark. The coast redwood's native range is limited to a thin coastal zone, rarely extending more than 20 miles inland, from Monterey County in the south to extreme southwestern Oregon in the north. Fossils of the coast redwood date back 65 million years to the Cretaceous Period, when the tree coexisted with the dinosaurs in North America, Europe, and Asia. As Earth's climate became cooler and drier, the tree gradually retreated to its current range, where the mild Mediterranean climate and coastal fogs provide the humid environment that redwoods prefer. Although not as long-lived as their relatives the giant sequoias, coast redwoods live a long time—many attain 800 years of age, and some last a millennium. Redwood lumber has always been in great demand for timber, as the wood is durable, decay resistant, and easy to work. Most of San Francisco's Victorian homes were constructed from redwood. The wood has proven so popular over the years that over 95 percent of the old-growth redwood forests have been wiped out, with conservationists scrambling to preserve the rest.

GIANT SEQUOIA

Related to coast redwoods, giant sequoias are the second species of "big trees" in California. They do not grow as tall as the coast redwoods, but their trunks are much more massive—in fact, these trees are the largest living things on Earth. The world's most massive tree is believed to be the General Sherman tree in Sequoia National Park. This tree is 275 feet high and has a diameter at its base of over 36 feet (wider than many of San Francisco's city streets!). Giant sequoias are also notable for their long life span, with the oldest documented tree over 3,600 years. The wood of giant sequoias is extremely brittle, so it is of little use as lumber, as California's first lumberjacks discovered to their chagrin when, lusting after hundreds of thousands of potential board feet of timber, they often watched the massive trees shatter into unusable pieces when felled.

LOCATION: Garfield Park, near 25th and Harrison Sts. in the Mission (several large examples in this park)

Like the coast redwood, the giant sequoia has retreated over millions of years from a broad distribution over most of the Northern Hemisphere to a narrow range in California. Giant sequoias are today limited to sixty-six groves spread over a narrow, 250-mile band on the western slopes of the Sierra Nevada Mountains, from Placer County in the north to Tulare County in the south, at elevations of 5,000–7,500 feet.

WINDMILL PALM

LOCATION: 20th Street near Folsom St. in the Mission; also many examples on 17th St. between Alabama and Florida Sts. in the Mission

Windmill palms are the most cold tolerant of the palms, able to survive temperatures as low as 10° Fahrenheit. They can be found as far north as Vancouver (photographers seem to love taking pictures of them covered with snow). In fact, like San Franciscans, these trees tolerate just about everything: drought, pollution, poor soil, and wind—they are almost impossible to kill. That's the good news. The bad news is that these trees are not going to win any awards for looks. The trunk of the windmill palm is covered with dense hair–like fibers, and the fan–shaped leaves do not have the feathery grace of the Canary Island palm. Still, if you want that tropical effect and you do not have a green thumb, this is your palm. Windmill palms are native to eastern China and Taiwan.

Tristaniopsis laurina (formerly *Tristania laurina*)

SMALL-LEAF TRISTANIA

LOCATION: 317 Castro St./Market St. in the Castro; also at 738 Ashbury St./Frederick St. in Cole Valley

The small–leaf tristania is perhaps San Francisco's most successful small street tree. If you don't have a green thumb and you need to plant a tree under utility wires, you can't do better than this one. It is a tough, hardy tree, resistant to disease and pests and tolerant of poor soils and wind. It doesn't need much care once established—it produces little leaf drop, and it needs relatively light pruning. These virtues have pushed this tree to #4 in the ranks of San Francisco's most popular street trees.

Small-leaf tristanias grow slowly to 20–25 feet in height. The narrow 4-inch leaves are medium green and glossy; semishowy yellow flowers bloom from April to June, followed by small (1/4–inch) seed capsules that drop during winter storms.

DON'T DO THIS!

Indulge me as I rant about two of my gripes concerning trees in San Francisco. The city has its share of beautiful trees, but there are times I walk down a street and cringe. If I could change only two things about what happens to trees in the city, these would be the two:

• LAVENDER IN THE TREE BASIN. Most street trees in San Francisco are planted as young trees in 2-foot-square cuts in the sidewalk, and people have a natural desire to plant flowers or other plants in the basins. Anything planted there will compete with the young tree just getting established, but plants with woody stems, such as lavender, rosemary, and ivy, are especially bad. Mature trees are not affected much, but the aggressive roots of these plants can choke a young tree by competing for water and nutrients.

• AGGRESSIVE PRUNING. Why are so many San Franciscans afraid to let their trees grow? Trees are "topped" or aggressively pruned for many reasons, chiefly to keep the treetop out of overhead wires and to protect views. But I suspect many tree owners think they are helping the tree by

lopping off the ends of branches to reduce the tree's height or size, or to make the tree bushier or denser. Some plants react well to being cut back hard in this way, but most trees are not among them. Take my advice: let your tree grow, and help create a mature canopy your neighbors will appreciate.

CHINESE ELM

The Chinese elm is by far the most common elm on San Francisco streets. A medium- to large-sized tree (growing 30–35 feet), it keeps its leaves year-round in San Francisco's mild climate and develops an attractive weeping form as it matures. The 1–2-inch leaves are smaller than those on other urban elms; this elm is also distinguished by bark that sheds in patches, creating beautiful two-toned (gray and brown) mottled patterns. Chinese elms are resistant to Dutch elm disease, which has decimated the American elm in most of the United States. San Francisco elms have not yet been affected by Dutch elm disease, and you can still find American elms here and there in the city. The Chinese elm is native to northern China, Japan, and Korea.

LOCATION: 720 Castro St./Liberty St. in the Castro; also at 245–255 Hartford St./19th St. in the Castro; many examples on both sides of Folsom St. between 24th and 26th Sts. in the Mission

MEXICAN FAN PALM

LOCATION: Mission Street between 15th and 16th Sts. in the Mission; also at 315 Arkansas St./18th St. on Potrero Hill (a very tall specimen that retains all its dead fronds)

This is one of the classic palms of California—in fact, it is said to be California's most common ornamental palm. There is no mistaking a mature Mexican fan palm—the tree's narrow 12–18-inch trunk can reach 100 feet in height, ending in a "feather duster" cap of palm fronds. In the wild, the palm thatch lasts many years before eventually falling off. In cultivation, the palm fronds can be cut near their base to create a crosshatched look, or trimmed further to create a smooth trunk. Because of their unique proportions, Mexican fan palms are frequently used to provide vertical accenting for streets or buildings. When young, this tree is hard to distinguish from the California fan palm (*Washingtonia filifera*), although as it ages the California fan palm develops a much wider trunk than its relative. The Mexican fan palm is native to marshes and riparian valleys in Baja California and northwest Mexico.

walking tours

SAN FRANCISCO IS A WALKER'S CITY. With its interesting architecture and unique neighborhoods, the city rewards even directionless meanders. A bit of knowledge about San Francisco's more common street trees can add to the pleasure of a city walk for locals and visitors alike, as each block in the urban forest contains its own unique mix of the familiar and mysterious.

Described here are several walkable (in some cases, bikeable) tours that will take you past notable trees in neighborhoods that offer interesting strolls even without the trees. Although the tours focus mainly on the trees, I point out other items of interest where they come up along the way.

I hope you will enjoy these walks. Most of all, I hope they will open your eyes to trees that will help you enjoy your everyday strolls around the beautiful city of San Francisco.

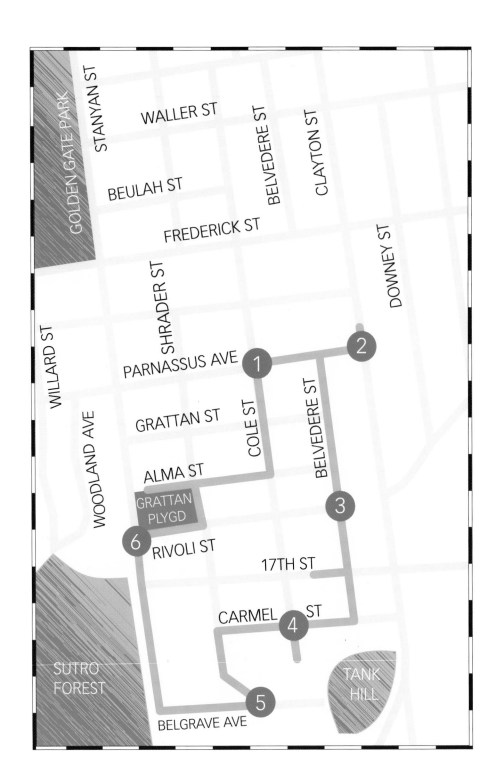

GOLDEN GATE PARK

STANYAN ST

WALLER ST

BELVEDERE ST

CLAYTON ST

BEULAH ST

FREDERICK ST

SHRADER ST

DOWNEY ST

WILLARD ST

PARNASSUS AVE

WOODLAND AVE

GRATTAN ST

COLE ST

BELVEDERE ST

ALMA ST

GRATTAN PLYGD

RIVOLI ST

17TH ST

CARMEL ST

SUTRO FOREST

TANK HILL

BELGRAVE AVE

COLE VALLEY

One of the best-treed neighborhoods in the city, this compact neighborhood boasts a great diversity of tree species for an area its size.

1 Start this tour at the corner of Cole St. and Parnassus Ave., where you'll see several **CAROB TREES** (*Ceratonia siliqua*), the best and largest at 957 Cole. Walk east to the two large trees at 58–60 Parnassus, and crush one of their leaves in your hand—the distinctive smell will identify these as **GRECIAN LAUREL**, or **SWEET BAY** (*Laurus nobilis*). I was recently doing some online research for a neighborhood tour I conduct that would involve a stop at these Parnassus Ave. trees, and to my amazement I discovered a quote from the Roman poet Virgil in his *Georgics*, from 29 B.C.: "Beneath its mother's mighty shade upshoots the bay-tree of Parnassus."

2 Continue up Parnassus Ave. to Clayton St., and turn left. At 893 Clayton (on your left as you face the house) is a **NORTHERN RATA** (*Metrosideros robusta*), side by side with a close relative, the more common **NEW ZEALAND CHRISTMAS TREE** (*Metrosideros excelsus*) (the tree on your right). This northern rata is one of only two examples of its species in the city that I know of outside Golden Gate Park. Turn around and head back to Belvedere St., one of the best-treed streets in San Francisco. Look up Belvedere for an example of how mature trees can enhance a streetscape. In the 1980s, this street had its overhead wires placed underground, which has allowed the trees to grow without excessive pruning.

3 Walk up Belvedere St. to nos. 466–468, where there are two graceful **CHINESE ELMS** (*Ulmus parvifolia*). Continue up Belvedere, passing a couple of **LEMONWOODS** (*Pittosporum eugenioides*) at nos. 516 and 575, and turn right on 17th St. At 4736 17th is a spectacular specimen (best in San Francisco) of **CORK OAK** (*Quercus suber*). (Push your fingers into the crevices of the bark to feel the spongy cork.) Turn around and head back up 17th to Belvedere and turn right. At 601 Belvedere is the former **ST. AIDAN'S EPISCOPAL CHURCH**, now converted to a private home. (The Grateful Dead practiced here in the 1960s, shortly after the building was decommissioned as a church.) Continue up Belvedere to the corner of Carmel St. Look left to the end of Carmel and you'll see another conversion— a former firehouse that was converted in the 1990s into two condos (complete with a preserved fire pole in one of them). Turn right at Carmel, and then left on Cole St. This dead-end block of Cole has several **CALLERY PEARS** (*Pyrus calleryana*), all planted at the same time in 1992, with the best at 1515 Cole.

4 Head back down Cole St. to Carmel and turn left. At 144 Carmel is a heavily pruned **Catalina ironwood** (*Lyonothamnus floribundus* ssp. *asplenifolius*), the only California native on this tour. Turn left again on Shrader St. At 1591 Shrader, stop and view the wooden sculpture of an angel just to the left of the driveway. This is the former home of socialite and philanthropist Pat Montandon. The sculpture, which Montandon titled *Angel of Hope*, was carved out of the trunk of a huge Monterey cypress by sculptor Jack Mealy. The tree had to come down after a companion Monterey cypress on the other side of the driveway fell over in a 1997 windstorm, and Montandon decided to commission the sculpture rather than cut the tree down to the ground.

5 Continue up Shrader St. to Belgrave Ave. If you have some time, turn left and follow the trail at the end of Belgrave to the top of Tank Hill for what is, in my opinion, the most spectacular panoramic view of San Francisco in the city. Notice the towering **blue gum** (*Eucalyptus globulus*) trees surrounding the foundation of the old water tank at the top of this hill—there were several more nearby until the city began a controversial project to cut down the trees to promote native vegetation on the hill (see page 64). Retrace your steps back to Belgrave Ave. (or just turn right on Belgrave if you've skipped Tank Hill). Follow Belgrave west to the beautiful garden at 160 Belgrave, where you'll see a **strawberry tree** (*Arbutus unedo*) in a yard in front of one of the largest **Japanese maples** (*Acer palmatum*) in San Francisco. Continue to the corner of Belgrave and Stanyan Sts., near where Belgrave dead-ends into Sutro Forest. This is a magical spot—the eucalyptus forest looming to the west, a bluish gray **Atlas cedar** (*Cedrus atlantica* 'Glauca') next to a charming cottage at 200 Belgrave, a spectacular view north to San Francisco Bay, and two towering **Norfolk Island pines** (*Araucaria heterophylla*) to the east at 190 Belgrave. Walk down the steep stairs of Stanyan St., past dozens of mature **American sweetgums** (*Liquidambar styraciflua*), until you pass 17th St. Among tree cognoscenti, the **New Zealand Christmas tree** (*Metrosideros excelsus*) at 1221 Stanyan is one of the city's most loved trees (see pages 20 and 69 to find out why).

6 Continue down Stanyan and turn right on Rivoli St. The half-modern building at the corner of Rivoli and Shrader Sts. (1401 Shrader) is the work of local architect Ira Kurlander, and the house (the first floor is a 1908 Edwardian) was formerly owned by Jerry Brown's mother, Bernice Lane Brown. (Notice the 10-foot-wide home designed by Kurlander in 2003, just a few steps up the hill on Shrader.) Turn left on Shrader and left on Alma St. to 246 Alma, where you'll find a very rare **EMPRESS TREE** *(Paulownia tomentosa)* with large leaves, and purple flowers in season. Backtrack on Alma, crossing Shrader St., to the **TOBIRA** *(Pittosporum tobira)* at 131 Alma—be sure to smell the flowers, which are powerfully fragrant. Continue to Cole St., turn left, and walk 2 blocks to Parnassus Ave., to where you began.

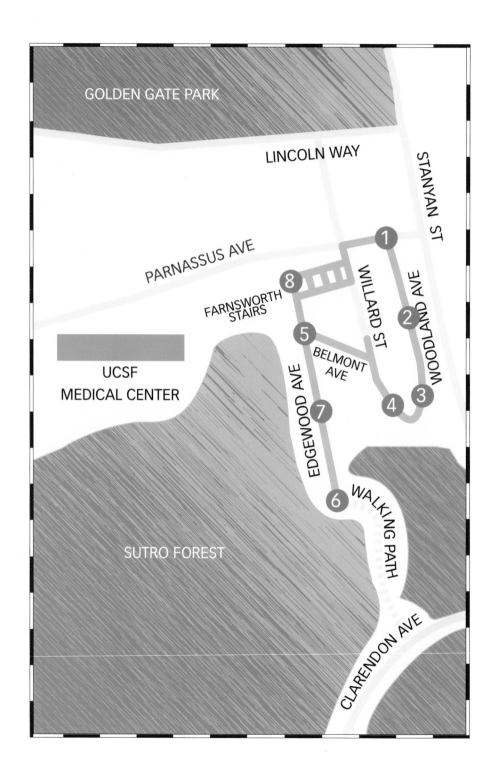

GOLDEN GATE PARK

LINCOLN WAY

STANYAN ST

PARNASSUS AVE

WILLARD ST

WOODLAND AVE

FARNSWORTH STAIRS

BELMONT AVE

EDGEWOOD AVE

UCSF
MEDICAL CENTER

WALKING PATH

SUTRO FOREST

CLARENDON AVE

PARNASSUS HEIGHTS

This tiny subneighborhood of San Francisco is composed of only four short streets nestled into the Sutro Forest near the University of California Medical Center.

This neighborhood is best known for the PURPLE-LEAF PLUMS that line its streets. In early February, Parnassus Heights is ablaze in pink flowers as the dense plantings of two varieties of plum—*Prunus cerasifera* 'Pissardii' and *Prunus* x *blireiana*—combine to put on a springtime show. Parnassus Heights is the home of Armistead Maupin, author of *Tales of the City* (and I live here, too).

1 Start this tour at the corner of Woodland and Parnassus Aves. Walk up Woodland to no. 15 to see an ATLAS CEDAR (*Cedrus atlantica* 'Glauca'), a bluish green cedar native to Algeria and northern Africa. At 25 Woodland is a SILVER DOLLAR GUM (*Eucalyptus polyanthemos*). These two trees help demonstrate how attractive large trees can be on streets without overhead utility wires—Woodland Ave. had its wires placed underground in the mid–1980s. At 20 Woodland is a SMALL-LEAF TRISTANIA (*Tristaniopsis laurina*), one of the hardiest street tree species in San Francisco.

2 Continue to 34 Woodland to see a well-maintained willow-like MAYTEN (*Maytenus boaria*), and to no. 58, where you'll find a NEW ZEALAND CHRISTMAS TREE (*Metrosideros excelsus*). This particular tree is a favorite of the "wild parrots of Telegraph Hill" (see page 32 for the full story); the parrots visit Parnassus Heights during July and August each year, and they love to munch this tree's red, bottle-brush-like flowers during the summer blooming season. At 78 Woodland are several large ENGLISH ELMS (*Ulmus procera*), and next door, at no. 90, are two well-maintained ITALIAN STONE PINES (*Pinus pinea*). Native to southern Europe and Turkey, Italian stone pines produce the pine nuts of Mediterranean cooking. The modest house at this address was built in 1936 by celebrated modernist architect Richard Neutra. It is one of only three Neutra homes in San Francisco.

3 Pass the rambling Psi Omega dental fraternity on your right at 101 Woodland Ave., with a particularly nice PURPLE-LEAF PLUM (*Prunus cerasifera*) in front. Then stop at the corner of Woodland Ave. and Willard St., where you'll see several ENGLISH HAWTHORNS (*Crataegus laevigata*). Facing south, you'll also have an excellent view of Sutro Forest, topped by the red-and-white Sutro Tower. The forest was planted in the late 1800s by Adolph Sutro, a silver magnate, large landowner (at one time he owned one-twelfth of the city's acreage), and mayor of San Francisco at the turn of the twentieth century.

4 Turn right onto Willard St. At 472–474 Willard is a **GIANT DRACAENA** (*Cordyline australis*), also called **CABBAGE PALM.** Not a true palm, it is from the agave family, related to the yuccas. Backtrack up Willard and turn right on Belmont Ave. With your back to 16 Belmont, look across the street at three large California native conifers, side by side: from the left: **MONTEREY CYPRESS** (*Cupressus macrocarpa*); **COAST REDWOOD** (*Sequoia sempervirens*); and **MONTEREY PINE** (*Pinus radiata*). The attractive house at 1 Belmont was built in 1904 over an old city reservoir and survived the 1906 earthquake.

5 Turn left on Edgewood Ave. and note the handsome brick paving up and down this street. At 206 Edgewood is one of the city's finest examples of **GRECIAN LAUREL**, or **SWEET BAY** (*Laurus nobilis*). Next door, just up the street, is a **LEMON BOTTLEBRUSH** (*Callistemon citrinus*). The house at 226 Edgewood was built in 1911 by Louis Christian Mullgardt, a California architect who also designed the original de Young museum in Golden Gate Park. In the yard at this address is a **GINKGO TREE** (*Ginkgo biloba*), and at no. 254 there is a large **BLACK WALNUT TREE** (*Juglans nigra*).

6 Walk to the end of Edgewood Ave. (passing the house at no. 278, which was designed by Julia Morgan, the architect of Hearst Castle), where you'll dead–end into the Sutro Forest. The forest, owned by the University of California, is now mainly a monoculture of **BLUE GUMS** (*Eucalyptus globulus*). Blue gums are the most common eucalyptus in rural California, but they are too large, messy, and brittle for urban streets. The forest was originally planted with eucalyptus, ash, pine, and cypress, but the eucalyptus eventually took over and crowded out the others. The trees are now reaching the end of their natural lives, and the university is currently studying what to do with the forest. If you're up for a stroll through the forest, follow the footpath at the end of Edgewood; if you keep left, the path will lead you to Clarendon Ave. after a 20–minute walk.

7 Turn around and head back to 218 Edgewood, where you'll see a **RED FLOW-ERING GUM** (*Corymbia ficifolia*). The view of San Francisco Bay from here, framed by the numerous purple-leaf plums, is one of my favorites.

8 Continue down to 185 Edgewood, where a rare **JAPANESE CRYPTOMERIA** (*Cryptomeria japonica*) stands next to the large **DEODAR CEDAR** (*Cedrus deodara*) at no. 183. At 110 Edgewood is a **FLOWERING ASH** (*Fraxinus ornus*), another rare species in San Francisco. Pause at the end of the street to take in the sweeping city and bay views, then turn right, down the charming Farnsworth stairs. If you're descending in summer, you'll enjoy a series of sensory delights as you pass a wild bramble of climbing roses, blackberries, and fruit-bearing plum trees. At the bottom of the stairs, turn left to find one of San Francisco's largest **VICTORIAN BOX TREES** (*Pittosporum undulatum*) at 1403 Willard St. Continue down Willard and turn right on Parnassus Ave., to return to your starting point at Woodland Ave.

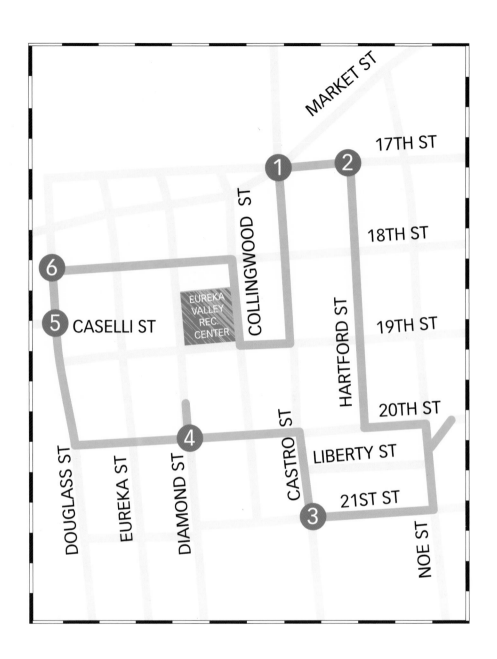

MARKET ST

17TH ST

18TH ST

19TH ST

20TH ST

COLLINGWOOD ST

HARTFORD ST

EUREKA VALLEY REC. CENTER

CASELLI ST

CASTRO ST

LIBERTY ST

21ST ST

DOUGLASS ST

EUREKA ST

DIAMOND ST

NOE ST

CASTRO/EUREKA VALLEY

This neighborhood, which has a nationwide reputation as the center of the city's gay and lesbian community, also has more than its fair share of landmark trees fronting the Victorian homes that line its streets.

This tour starts at the corner of 17th, Castro, and Market Sts. If you're visiting the city without a car or are just environmentally conscious, take the underground K, L, or M Muni lines up Market St. to the Castro station, where you'll emerge at this corner. (Drivers may want to try the much easier street parking near the 21st St. portion of the tour, starting the tour's loop from that point.) This walk has some steep hills, so be sure your legs are up for it before taking off on foot!

1 From the corner of 17th and Castro, look down at the string of **CANARY ISLAND PALMS** (*Phoenix canariensis*) that line Market below Castro. These trees were added when the popular F line historic streetcars were introduced in 1993. Palm trees are easy to transplant, and the trees on Market between Castro and Church Sts. came from yards in the San Francisco Peninsula—homeowners were glad to accept the city's offer to remove the trees, since after 25 or 30 years of their life span of 300+ years, the palms had become too large.

2 Head 1 block downhill (east) on 17th St. to Hartford St. **BRISBANE BOX** (*Lophostemon confertus*) trees are planted densely along 17th, and several are near this corner, including one in front of the gas station on your left, and a few at 3943–3947 17th. Turn right onto Hartford, where at no. 45 you'll see a beautiful **WASHINGTON THORN** (*Crataegus phaenopyrum*) that blooms in late May or June. Continue down Hartford past the many Victorian and Edwardian homes, including the Hartford Street Zen Center at no. 57. Just before you reach 18th St., on your left are four trees that alternate between **PURPLE-LEAF PLUM** (*Prunus cerasifera*) and **JAPANESE FLOWERING CHERRY** (*Prunus serrulata*). Cross 18th and continue up Hartford. At 245 and 255 Hartford are two large and spectacular **CHINESE ELMS** (*Ulmus parvifolia*). Turn left at 20th St. and right on Noe St., passing one of my favorite recent-construction buildings in the city, the neocraftsman-style structure at 702 Noe. At 740 Noe is a **GINKGO** (*Ginkgo biloba*) and, underneath it, a rare California native (in fact, a San Francisco native!), **HOLLYLEAF CHERRY** (*Prunus ilicifolia*). Turn left and head up 20th St.; across the street from the steep driveway next to 4085 20th is a rare **CORK OAK TREE**. Backtrack on 20th, turn left on Noe, and turn right on 21st St. At 3824 21st is a **RED FLOWERING GUM** (*Corymbia ficifolia*); at nos. 3875 and 3881 are the city's best specimens of **LAVALLE HAWTHORN** (*Crataegus* x *lavallei*).

3 Continue on 21st to Castro St. and turn right; you'll pass several more large **CALIFORNIA PEPPERS** on your right in the 700 block of Castro. At the corner of 20th St., the Queen Anne Victorian at 701 Castro is the former home of Fernando Nelson, probably the most prolific builder in San Francisco history. Nelson churned out over 4,000 Victorian and Edwardian homes during his lifetime. Turn left on 20th, cross Collingwood St., and at no. 4234 notice the old and gnarled **LEMON VERBENA** (*Aloysia triphylla*) shrub in the small garden (on your right as you face the house). The lemony oils from the leaves of this plant make it a popular flavoring for teas and iced drinks.

4 Turn right on Diamond St. and head downhill to no. 281, where there's a **BRUSH CHERRY** (*Syzygium paniculatum*). Backtrack up Diamond and turn right onto 20th St. When you cross Eureka St., look down the hill at the row of beautiful **GINKGOS** (*Ginkgo biloba*) at 250–278 Eureka. Continue up 20th St., where in the yard at no. 4521 you'll find a **NORFOLK ISLAND PINE** (*Araucaria heterophylla*) and, just below it, a well-maintained **CAMPHOR TREE** (*Cinnamomum camphora*). At 4536 20th is an attractive **EVERGREEN PEAR** (*Pyrus kawakamii*). Turn right at the bend and head down Douglass St. At 325–327 Douglass, two **RED FLOWER-ING GUMS** reach down to street level, where you can easily see the flowers (in season) and bowl-shaped seed pods. Farther down the street at 284 Douglass is a rare **GOLDEN RAIN TREE** (*Koelreuteria paniculata*).

5 Stop at the corner of Caselli St. The oversized Victorian building here, at 250 Douglass, is the Nobby Clarke mansion, an oversized Queen Anne/Classical Revival building constructed in 1891 when it lorded over an 18-acre property; it was later converted into a hospital and now has been subdivided into apartments. On Caselli fronting this property are several large **NICHOL'S WILLOW-LEAFED PEPPERMINT TREES** (*Eucalyptus nicholii*).

6 Continue on Douglass and turn right onto 18th St. You'll find an **ITALIAN BUCKTHORN** (*Rhamnus alaternus*) at 4445 18th and a **CAJEPUT** (*Melaleuca quinquenervia*) across the street at nos. 4438–4444. Walk 2 blocks down 18th St. to Diamond St., where on your right is Most Holy Redeemer Catholic Church, built in 1901 for a predominately Irish/German neighborhood and now serving a largely gay and lesbian congregation. Across Diamond St. from Most Holy Redeemer are two **NEW ZEALAND CHRISTMAS TREES** (*Metrosideros excelsus*). Continue down 18th St. to Collingwood St. and turn right. Across the street from 173–185 Collingwood are two **CAMPHOR TREES** (*Cinnamomum camphora*). Turn left on 19th St. At 4097–4099 19th are several large **CHINESE PHOTINIAS** (*Photinia serrulata*), the best in the city. Take a left, heading downhill on Castro St., and walk the colorful commercial strip of this neighborhood (note especially the memorial to Harvey Milk at 573–575 Castro) to return to your starting place at 17th St.

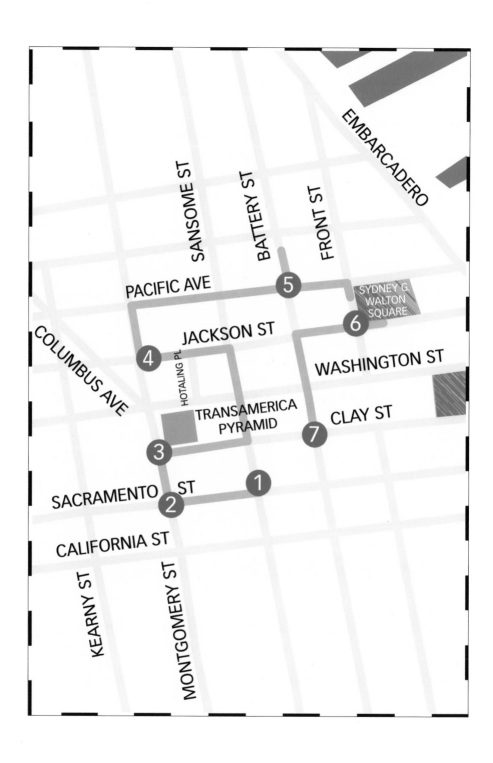

SANSOME ST

BATTERY ST

FRONT ST

EMBARCADERO

PACIFIC AVE

5

SYDNEY G.
WALTON
SQUARE

6

JACKSON ST

COLUMBUS AVE

4

HOTALING PL

WASHINGTON ST

TRANSAMERICA
PYRAMID

CLAY ST

3

7

SACRAMENTO ST

1

2

CALIFORNIA ST

KEARNY ST

MONTGOMERY ST

FINANCIAL DISTRICT

Surprisingly, the Financial District of San Francisco is home to some of the city's most impressive trees. This tour will also take you through the adjacent Jackson Square district, with its blocks and blocks of intact pre-earthquake architecture.

1 Start the tour in front of the colossal Ionic columns of the old Federal Reserve Bank at 400 Sansome St., near Sacramento St. Built in 1924, this building is a great example of the classic banking "temples" of the early twentieth century. The building is surrounded by some of the finest TULIP TREES (*Liriodendron tulipifera*) in the city, with the two best fronting the Sansome St. entrance.

2 Walk west on Sacramento St. to Montgomery St., turn right, and walk 1 block, stopping under the landmark Transamerica Pyramid, San Francisco's tallest building and the "exclamation point" in the city's skyline. Built in 1972, the building's origin can be traced to trees, according to the Transamerica Corporation website:

> It all began in 1968 when [Transamerica] President John R. Beckett noticed that the trees in a city park—unlike the surrounding, box-like buildings—allowed natural light and fresh air to filter down to the streets below. Wishing to achieve the same effect with Transamerica's new headquarters, an unconventional pyramid shape was chosen for the building.

3 Turn right to walk along Clay St. in front of the Pyramid. You'll pass alternating SPOTTED GUM (*Eucalyptus maculata*) and RED FLOWERING GUM (*Corymbia ficifolia*), both Australian imports. The spotted gum is rare in San Francisco, and these here are some of the best in the city. Midblock you'll pass Redwood Park—a half-acre grove of COAST REDWOODS (*Sequoia sempervirens*) that was Transamerica Corporation's gift to the city. Redwoods thrive best in coastal valleys, sheltered from the wind, and these trees seem to be flourishing next to their gigantic windbreak to the west. Continue on Clay St. to Sansome St., turn left, and follow Sansome across Washington St. On the left in the middle of the next block are several NEW ZEALAND CHRISTMAS TREES (*Metrosideros excelsus*). Turn left on Jackson St., where you'll find a beautiful tree–lined block of pre–earthquake architecture. At 406 Jackson is a large, deciduous CALLERY PEAR (*Pyrus calleryana*). Midblock you'll see Hotaling Pl. on your left, where wavy lines in the cement mark the original shoreline in this part of the city. A historical marker on the building at the corner notes that the building, which was the largest liquor repository for gold rush–era San Francisco, survived the 1906 earthquake and fire, inspiring Charles Field's famous doggerel: "If, as they say, God spanked the town for being over frisky, Why did he burn his churches down and save Hotaling's whisky?"

4 Continue on Jackson St. On your right, at 494 and 498 Jackson, are two of the best-kept GINKGOS (*Ginkgo biloba*) in San Francisco. Turn right on Montgomery St. and walk 1 block to Pacific Ave. On the far left corner you'll find excellent examples of two related kinds of bottlebrush trees—at 500 Pacific, two large WEEPING BOTTLEBRUSH (*Callistemon viminalis*), and around the corner at 909 Montgomery, a more rounded LEMON BOTTLEBRUSH (*Callistemon citrinus*). Turn right on Pacific, and continue on that street to no. 323, where you'll pass several OLIVE TREES (*Olea europaea*).

5 At Battery St., turn left. Just past No. 712, several EVERGREEN PEARS (*Pyrus kawakamii*) rise out of a sunken parking lot; note their arching, graceful branches and fractured, charcoal-colored bark. Backtrack on Battery, passing the giant anchor on your left that marks the Old Ship Saloon at the corner of Battery and Pacific—reputed to be the oldest bar in San Francisco. A saloon has been on this site ever since 1851, when a gold rush-era clipper ship that had been deliberately beached on this spot was converted into an impromptu bar by cutting a door into the side of the ship. Turn left on Pacific and cross Front St., then take a few steps to the right to the arch that marks the entrance to Sydney G. Walton Square, a 1-block oasis in the Financial District. The pines that ring the park are favorite roosting spots for San Francisco's wild parrots (see page 32)—look or listen for them here, especially near the end of the day. A BLUE ATLAS CEDAR (*Cedrus atlantica* 'Glauca') has been planted in the center of the park, where it will have plenty of room to grow.

6 Exit from the park to the right on Jackson St., turn right, and follow Jackson to Battery St., where you'll turn left. On your left you'll see two dozen **LONDON PLANE TREES** (*Platanus acerifolia*) that have been pollarded. Across Battery, lining the impressive U.S. Customs House, are several large **GRECIAN BAY TREES** (*Laurus nobilis*), including San Francisco's largest.

7 Continue on Battery St. to the corner of Clay St., where this tour ends with a great view of two notable pieces of San Francisco architecture: on your right, the Transamerica Pyramid; on your left, the brown, crosshatched One Maritime Plaza, one of the first buildings anywhere to put its seismic braces on its exterior.

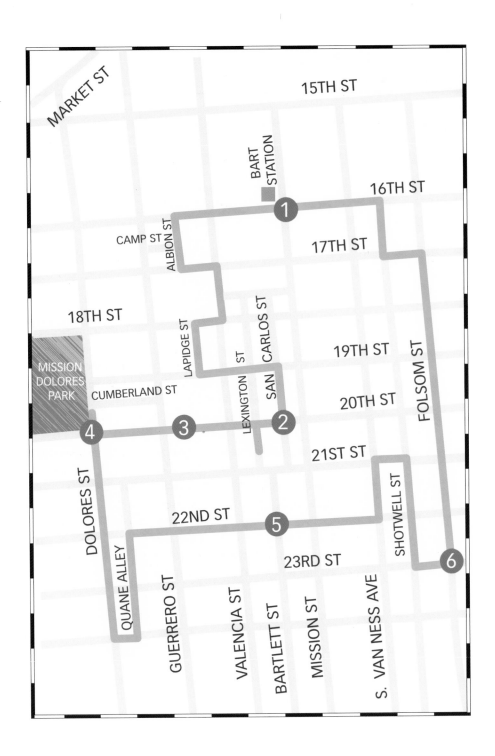

THE MISSION

The Mission has some of the best conditions for trees in San Francisco, with good soils and less wind and fog than in the rest of the city. You'll find many trees here that exist nowhere else in San Francisco.

We start this walk at the BART station at 16th and Mission Sts., to make it an easy car-free tour. This tour makes an ideal bike trip, since the route is relatively flat.

1 From the BART station, walk west on 16th St., past Valencia St. to Albion St., and turn left. This tiny street has some of the most impressive melaleuca trees in the city—you'll walk past FLAXLEAF PAPERBARKS (*Melaleuca linarifolia*) at nos. 166–168 and 170, and a PRICKLY MELALEUCA (*Melaleuca styphelioides*) at nos. 194–196. (Midblock, at the corner of Albion and Camp Sts., a bronze plaque marks the spot of the original Mission Dolores, where Spanish explorers first camped on June 27, 1776.) Continue on Albion St., turn left on 17th St., then right on Valencia. (Clarion Alley, on your left across the street, is worth a short detour for its end-to-end murals.) At 696 Valencia are two SILK OAKS (*Grevillea robusta*); turn right to find another at 3820 18th St. Continue on 18th to Lapidge St. At the corner of 18th and Lapidge is the Women's Building, a cultural and educational center that is a Mission neighborhood landmark. Turn left on Lapidge to 19th St., and turn left on 19th St. The trees nearest the corner at 3505 19th are CHINABERRY TREES (*Melia azedarach*), a very rare tree in San Francisco. If you're visiting in May or June, you'll see their attractive lavender flowers. Cross Valencia St. at this corner and walk east on 19th, past Lexington St. to San Carlos St., then turn right. On this block of San Carlos you'll see two warmth-loving trees, thriving in the sunny Mission. At no. 226 is a JACARANDA (*Jacaranda mimosifolia*), a native of Brazil, and at nos. 237–239 is an Australian native, a LEMON-SCENTED GUM (*Corymbia citriodora*). Both these trees are limited in their San Francisco range to a few neighborhoods on the warmer, eastern side of the city.

2 Follow San Carlos St. to the corner of 20th St., turn right, then turn left on Lexington St., which is a rare, intact example of nineteenth-century speculative-built housing in San Francisco. A developer built a row of nearly identical Italianate Victorians on the street in 1876; you can still see a few of them (at nos. 346–348 and 352–354) with their original front yards and iron fences. Lexington has a large **WHITE MULBERRY** (*Morus alba*), the tree on which silkworms feed, at no. 330. Backtrack on Lexington to 20th St.; turn left, where you'll find a **NORFOLK ISLAND PINE** (*Araucaria heterophylla*) that seems perfect between the two ornate Victorians at 3625 and 3635 20th St. Continue on 20th St., and notice how most of the houses on the left side of 20th St. are pre-1906 Victorian in style, while most of those on the right side are post-1906 Edwardians. The reason? The great fire that followed the 1906 earthquake was stopped in the Mission District at 20th St.

3 Continue to the **CAROB TREE** (*Ceratonia siliqua*) at 3733–3735 20th St. Unlike most carobs in the city, this is a female tree, producing the long, leathery pods that are ground into carob, a chocolate substitute. Continue up to Dolores St. and turn right. At the Christian Science church just before Cumberland St., turn left and cross Dolores St. In Dolores Park in front of you, next to a beautiful grove of **FAN PALMS** (*Washingtonia* sp.), are three large **BALD CYPRESS** (*Taxodium distichum*), some of the best specimens in San Francisco. Now walk uphill (south) on Dolores St. and notice the many palm trees, mostly **CANARY ISLAND PALMS** (*Phoenix canariensis*) in the center median as you go. Wild parrots nest in many of these palms—the birds are colorful and loud, so they'll be easy to spot if they're nearby. The flock here is a different group than the Telegraph Hill flock described on page 32.

4 At 20th and Dolores Sts., a beautiful row of **SOUTHERN MAGNOLIAS** (*Magnolia grandiflora*) lines the edge of Dolores Park. Continue on Dolores St.; between nos. 907 and 915 are a pair of **FICUS TREES** (*Ficus microcarpa*), perhaps San Francisco's most common street tree. Continue to 1073–1075 Dolores, where you'll see a rare **LILY-OF-THE-VALLEY TREE** (*Crinodendron patagua*), the only one I know of on San Francisco's streets. Turn left on 24th St. and left again on Quane Alley, where a large **AMERICAN ELM** (*Ulmus americana*) is on your right mid-block, across from a whimsical Calvin & Hobbes mural. Take Quane past 23rd to 22nd St., and turn right. On your left at 3456 22nd is one of the largest **PEPPERMINT WILLOWS** (*Agonis flexuosa*) in San Francisco. Continue on 22nd; the 3300 block of 22nd St.

has one of the city's most beautiful rows of GINKGOS (*Ginkgo biloba*) on your left as you descend. Coming to Valencia St., you'll see the Italian grocery Lucca Ravioli (at 1100 Valencia), a Mission District institution that has been in continuous operation since 1917.

5 Continue down 22nd to Bartlett St., which has ROBINIAS to either side– *Robinia* x *ambigua* on the left, and older BLACK LOCUSTS (*Robinia pseudoacacia*) on the right. Stay on 22nd St., passing the former Evangelical Lutheran St. Johannes Church, converted in the 1990s to a private residence, and soon to become a Buddhist temple. (Note the cornerstone inscribed in German, a relic of this formerly German/Irish neighborhood.) Turn left on South Van Ness Ave., and stop at 1011 S. Van Ness to see one of the city's best AVOCADOS (*Persea americana*). Turn right on 21st St. and right again onto a leafy block of Shotwell St., lined with LONDON PLANE TREES (*Platanus* x *acerifolia*). Continue on Shotwell, past César Chávez Elementary School (notice the beautiful murals), to 23rd St. and turn left. On the west side of the street, behind a tall fence, is a property that has been a communal dwelling since the 1960s. The commune tends a small orchard over the fence, with grapefruit, orange, and avocado trees. The group also planted the food–producing SPANISH CHESTNUTS (*Castanea sativa*) and ALMOND TREES (*Prunus dulcis*) fronting the property (the only examples of each that I know of on San Francisco streets).

6 Follow 23rd St. to Folsom St. and turn left. Folsom from here to 21st St. has been lined with graceful CHINESE ELMS (*Ulmus parvifolia*). At the far right corner of Folsom and 20th St., several WINDMILL PALMS (*Trachycarpus fortunei*) grace a mural in the background. Between 19th and 18th Sts., Folsom has a number of RED FLOWERING GUMS (*Corymbia ficifolia*), but on the right, in mid–block, is a large SPOTTED GUM (*Eucalyptus maculata*), which has been severely pruned but still sports beautifully mottled bark. Continue on Folsom St. to 17th St. and turn left. The parking lot to your right is surrounded in an alternating pattern by several types of trees that are very rare in San Francisco, including FLOSS SILK TREES (*Chorisia speciosa* 'Majestic Beauty'), with thorns on the trunk; FLAME TREES (*Brachychiton acerifolius*), with large, lobed leaves resembling fig leaves; BOTTLE TREES (*Brachychiton populneus*), with smaller leaves and a large trunk at the base; and MOUNTAIN SHE–OAKS (*Casuarina stricta*), with long, pinelike needles. Turn right onto Shotwell St., continue on Shotwell to 16th St., turn left, and continue back to the starting point at Mission St.

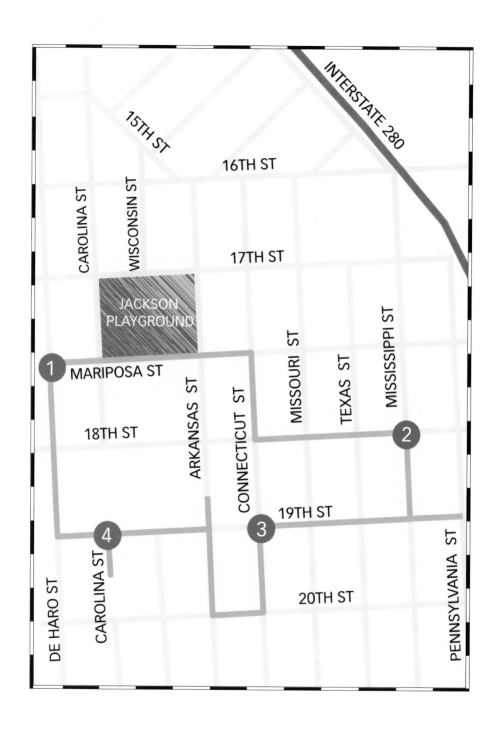

POTRERO HILL

Potrero Hill has neighborhood charm, steep hills, and San Francisco's sunniest and warmest weather—you'll see warmth-loving trees here that are rare in the rest of the city.

Start at the corner of De Haro and Mariposa Sts. If you notice a hoppy smell as you approach this corner, don't be surprised; the large industrial building at 1705 Mariposa is the historic Anchor Brewing Co. brewery, where Anchor Steam beer is made. (When you're not taking a tree tour, I recommend the brewery tour.)

1 Walk east on Mariposa to the corner of Carolina St., where to your left on the border of the Jackson playground are two of the city's largest **OLIVE TREES** (*Olea europeae*). Continue on Mariposa past several **QUEEN PALMS** (*Syagrus romanzofianum*), on your right, to the corner of Arkansas St.; look right and notice the row of large healthy **FICUS** (*Ficus microcarpa*). Ficus are notorious for breaking sidewalks, and here you'll see that pains have been taken to accommodate their roots; many of these trees have been sensibly planted with large, 8–foot basins paved with nonmortared bricks. Walk another block on Mariposa St., turn right on Connecticut St., and continue to no. 227, where there is a **EUROPEAN HORN-BEAM** (*Carpinus betulus* 'Fastigiata')—it is not a common tree in San Francisco, and this is one of the city's best. Continue up Connecticut and take a left on 18th St. Just uphill from 1424 18th, look over the fence to view the gigantic leaves and (if the season is right) equally gigantic purple flowers of a large **WIGANDIA URENS** (a native of South America) in a backyard. Continue on 18th St. (you might pause at no. 1315 for refreshment at Farleys, a favorite neighborhood coffee-house) to no. 1299, where you'll find an **EVERGREEN PEAR** (*Pyrus kawakamii*).

2 Follow 18th St. to Mississippi St., turn right, and stop at 321–323 Mississippi for a large **BRUSH CHERRY** (*Syzygium paniculatum*), directly across the street from an even larger **WHITE ALDER** (*Alnus rhombifolia*) at no. 328. Farther up Mississippi, look left at the corner of 19th St. to see a stately **CANARY ISLAND PALM** (*Phoenix canariensis*) against the horizon in a yard at 400 Pennsylvania Ave. Turn left on 19th for a close-up view of the house, built in 1870 and one of the oldest on Potrero Hill. (Owned by the navy during World War II, the house was condemned in 1974 before being renovated in the late 1970s.) Pause for the spectacular view of downtown San Francisco and the bay at the intersection of Pennsylvania and 19th Sts., then backtrack and head 3 blocks west on 19th to the corner of Missouri St. At the southwest corner, in front of a converted church, you'll see one of the few **PRICKLY MELALEUCAS** (*Melaleuca styphelioides*) in San Francisco. Notice the papery whitish bark that comes off in sheets.

3 Continue on 19th St. to Connecticut St. Several California–native **CATALINA IRONWOODS** (*Lyonothamnus floribundus* ssp. *asplenifolius*) are on the Connecticut St. side of St. Teresa's Church at this corner. Turn left onto Connecticut and notice several **GLOSSY PRIVETS** (*Ligustrum lucidum*) between nos. 407 and 455 as you ascend the street. Turn right on 20th St. and right again on Arkansas St.; at 438–440 Arkansas is one of the city's best **AVOCADO TREES** (*Persea americana*), although, like most San Francisco trees, this one is without fruit. The east side of this block of Arkansas has a row of **LEMON BOTTLEBRUSH** (*Callistemon citrinus*). Continue down Arkansas to no. 319 for an olfactory surprise—a **SWEETSHADE TREE** (*Hymenosporum flavum*). If it is in bloom, smell the cream–colored blossoms— my favorite fragrance of all San Francisco's trees.

4 Backtrack to 19th St. and take a right, then walk 2 blocks and take a left on Carolina St. At 618 Carolina is a **JACARANDA** (*Jacaranda mimosifolia*); these warmth-loving trees thrive on sunny Portrero Hill. Turn back to 19th St., turn left, then right on De Haro. Walk past the modernist Enola Maxwell Middle School and a row of **LOMBARDY POPLARS** (*Populus nigra* 'Italica') on your right, and then the beautiful St. Gregory of Nyssa Church (built in 1995, when it won the American Institute of Architects award for best new religious building of the year) on your left to complete your Potrero Hill tour.

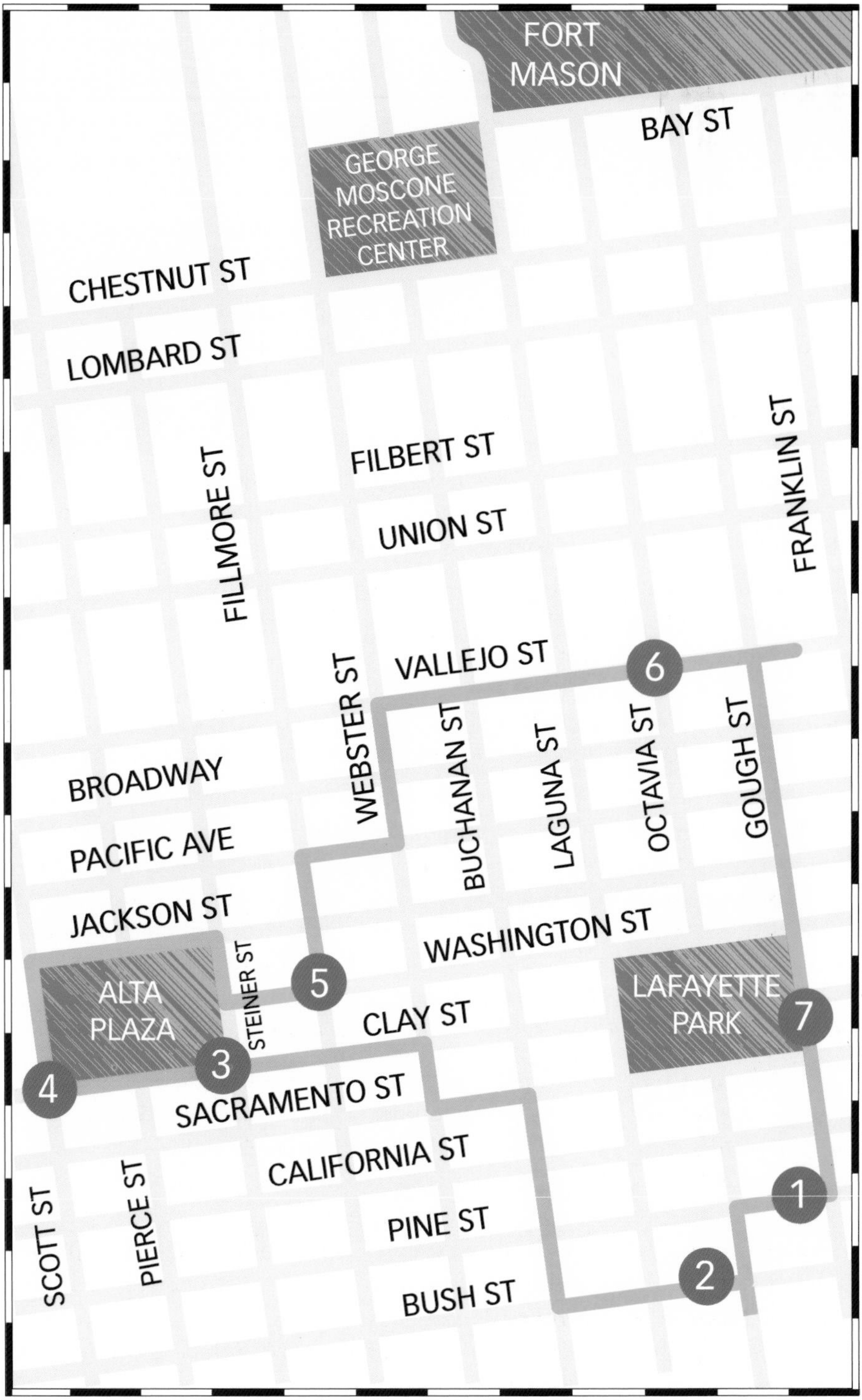
FORT MASON
BAY ST
GEORGE MOSCONE RECREATION CENTER
CHESTNUT ST
LOMBARD ST
FILLMORE ST
FILBERT ST
UNION ST
FRANKLIN ST
VALLEJO ST
WEBSTER ST
6
BUCHANAN ST
LAGUNA ST
OCTAVIA ST
GOUGH ST
BROADWAY
PACIFIC AVE
JACKSON ST
WASHINGTON ST
STEINER ST
5
ALTA PLAZA
LAFAYETTE PARK
7
CLAY ST
3
4
SACRAMENTO ST
CALIFORNIA ST
1
PINE ST
SCOTT ST
PIERCE ST
2
BUSH ST

PACIFIC HEIGHTS

Pacific Heights is one of San Francisco's toniest neighborhoods. You'll see some great trees on this tour, as well as some of the city's most interesting architecture. (The fire that destroyed much of San Francisco after the 1906 earthquake was stopped at the edge of Pacific Heights by dynamiting an entire block of Van Ness Ave.)

1 Start at 1701 Gough St., near the corner of Gough and Pine Sts., where a stately **NORFOLK ISLAND PINE** (*Araucaria heterophylla*) stands in a front yard. Walk west to Octavia St., to the edge of San Francisco's Japantown—the church ahead and on your right is St. Francis Xavier Church, a center for San Francisco's Japanese Catholics. Turn left on Octavia and cross Bush St.; on your right, you'll see a row of huge **BLUE GUMS** (*Eucalyptus globulus*). Note the sidewalk plaque here commemorating Mary Ellen Pleasant, the "Mother of Civil Rights in California," who planted these trees (see page 40 for her story).

2 Backtrack to Bush St., turn left, and walk 2 blocks to Buchanan St. Look left at the corner of Buchanan to see a block of Japantown full of **PURPLE-LEAF PLUMS** (*Prunus cerasifera*), which are planted heavily in this neighborhood. Turn right on Buchanan and walk to no. 1968, where you'll see the only **SAWLEAF ZELKOVA** (*Zelkova serrata*) I know of in San Francisco. Continue to 2050 Buchanan, where two **WHITE ALDERS** (*Alnus rhombifolia*) stand. Cross California St. and stop at 2155 Buchanan for a row of **RED FLOWERING GUMS** (*Corymbia ficifolia*), which may be in bloom if you're visiting in summertime. Turn left on Sacramento St.; at nos. 2305–2307 and 2315 are two **AUSTRALIAN TEA TREES** (*Leptospermum laevigatum*), and farther down the block, just past no. 2329, is a tall **AVOCADO** (*Persea americana*). Turn right on Webster St., and on your left, across the street from no. 2100, is a row of **GRECIAN LAUREL** or **SWEET BAY TREES**; these are the 'Saratoga' variety of *Laurus nobilis*. Turn left on Clay St. and cross Fillmore St.; between nos. 2549 and 2559 is a row of **SYDNEY GOLDEN WATTLES** (*Acacia longifolia*).

3 Continue on Clay past Steiner St.; Alta Plaza Park will now be on your right. We will walk around almost the entire border of this 4-square-block park, so feel free to duck into it at any point and enjoy its fine views. At 2643 Clay, an **OLIVE TREE** (*Olea europeae*) sits in a yard. Continue on Clay St., and on your left between nos. 2741 and 2799 is a row of **VICTORIAN BOX TREES** (*Pittosporum undulatum*)—if you can reach the flowers, stop to smell their orange blossom–like fragrance. At the corner of Clay and Scott Sts., look left to see one of the largest pollarded **LONDON PLANE TREES** (*Platanus x acerifolia*) in the city. (Pollarding is the process of pruning a tree at the same place each year, resulting in a swelling of the branch at the spot where the cut is made.)

4 Take a right on Scott St. In the park, across the street from 2221 Scott, is one of the city's larger **STRAWBERRY TREES** (*Arbutus unedo*). Continue to the corner of Jackson and Scott, where there is a giant **MONTEREY PINE** (*Pinus radiata*)—a California native and one of San Francisco's most common park trees. Take a right onto Jackson St. In the park across from 2510 and 2502 Jackson are several rare **PORT ORFORD CEDARS** (*Chamaecyparis lawsoniana*). At the corner of Jackson and Steiner Sts., look left to see the tall, handsome building at 2500 Steiner—one of the tallest buildings in Pacific Heights, with some of the best views in the city. Take a right on Steiner, passing some **DEODAR CEDARS** (*Cedrus deodara*) in the park across from 2420 Steiner, then turn left on Washington St. At 2561 Washington are a couple of **BLACKWOOD ACACIAS** (*Acacia melanoxylon*), a common tree in Pacific Heights. Continue to the corner of Fillmore St. and notice the abundance of **FICUS TREES** (*Ficus microcarpa*) near this corner. Like the blackwood acacia, ficus was heavily planted throughout the city until recently.

5 Take a left on Fillmore and walk 2 blocks, passing the shops and restaurants of the commercial heart of Pacific Heights. At 2529 Fillmore, notice the **CLUSTER PINE** (*Pinus pineaster*), then turn right on Pacific Ave. Continue on Pacific to no. 2301 to view several London plane trees that have been trained, or "espaliered," until they have fused together! Look east down Pacific—unless it's foggy, you'll be able to see the Bay Bridge far in the distance. Turn left on Webster St., passing the Italian consulate at no. 2590, and pause at Webster and Broadway to take in the view of the bay. Descend on Webster to Vallejo St. and take a right. Walk 1 block to Buchanan St. and notice a row of **LOMBARDY POPLARS** (*Populus nigra* 'Italica') running down Buchanan on your left. Continue on Vallejo to no. 2065, where a **NEW ZEALAND TEA TREE** (*Leptospermum scoparium*) is in a yard on your right. (Tea made from the leaves of this species helped save Captain Cook's sailors from scurvy as they were exploring Australia and New Zealand.)

6 Follow Vallejo to the corner of Octavia St., where on your right at 2522 Octavia is a rare (for San Francisco) **SPANISH FIR** (*Abies pinsapo*). Continue on Vallejo past Gough St. to the iron-gated Italianate Victorian home at 1772 Vallejo, where you'll find two examples of very rare trees in San Francisco. To the left of the driveway at this address is a **NORTHERN RATA** (*Metrosideros robusta*). In the yard to the right is one of my favorite trees in San Francisco—a gorgeous **TITOKI TREE** (*Alectryon excelsus*, a New Zealand native), and the only one I know of on San Francisco's streets. Backtrack to Gough, turn left, and walk 2 blocks; just before Pacific on your right are three stately **MEXICAN FAN PALMS** (*Washingtonia robusta*). Continue on Gough to Jackson St.; looking right at this corner you'll see a row of **STRAWBERRY TREES** (*Arbutus* 'Marina'), including several that front the German consulate at 1950–1960 Jackson.

7 As you continue on Gough, on your left in the next block behind a tall retaining wall is a **BIGLEAF MAPLE** (*Acer macrophyllum*), a California native. At 1850 Gough are two tall **NEW ZEALAND CHRISTMAS TREES** (*Metrosideros excelsus*) (on your right as you face this address). Continue 2 blocks further to that Norfolk Island pine at 1701 Gough St., where the tour began.

MAP OF SAN FRANCISCO

PRESIDIO

1

PACIFIC AVE

LYON ST

LOM

CALIFORNIA ST

CALIFORNIA ST

LYON ST

GEARY BLVD

GEARY BLVD

ANZA ST

ANZA ST

RICHMOND

SUTRO HTS AVE

STANYAN ST

UNIVERSITY OF
SAN FRANCISCO

PARK PRESIDIO BLVD

1

GOLDEN GATE PARK

HAIGHT ST

HAIGHT

1

40TH AVE

SUNSET BLVD

30TH AVE

24TH AVE

15TH AVE

JUDAH   PARNASSUS

STANYAN ST

CLAYTON ST

ASHBURY

VISTA W

COLE
VALLEY

17TH ST

UCSF
MEDICAL CENTER

40TH AVE

30TH AVE

24TH AVE

LAWTON ST

LAWTON ST

PARNASSUS
HEIGHTS

SUNSET

15TH AVE

7TH AVE

1

RIVERA ST

RIVERA ST

LAGUNA HONDA

FOREST
HILL

PORTOLA DR

SUNSET BLVD

30TH AVE

24TH AVE

19TH AVE

15TH AVE

WEST
PORTAL

VINCENTE

VINCENTE

VINCENTE

40TH AVE

SUNSET BLVD

WAWONA

WAWONA

WAWONA

WEST PORTAL AVE

YERBA BUENA A

SAN FRANCISCO
ZOO

SLOAT BLVD

OCEAN AVE

ST FRANCIS
WOOD

JOOST AVE

MONTEREY BLV

GREAT HIGHWAY

SKYLINE BLVD

LAKE MERCED BLVD

LAKE MERCED BL

LAKE MERCED

19TH AVE

JUNIPERO SERRA

OCEAN AVE

SAN JOSE A

SF STATE
UNIVERSITY

1

FONT BLV

OMI

CITY COLLEGE
OF SF

OCEAN AVE

SAN JOSE AV

MISSI

HOLLAWAY AVE

MIRAMAR AVE

HAROLD AVE

LAKE MERCED BLVD

FONT BLV

JOHN MUIR DR

SAN JOSE AV

280

1

the best trees

Following is a listing of the best trees on San Francisco's streets, in my (humble) opinion, grouped by neighborhood.

BAYVIEW/HUNTERS POINT

☐ *Acacia baileyana* (**BAILEY'S ACACIA**); 1700 block of Newhall St. between Revere Ave. and Bayview Ct.

☐ *Eucalyptus sideroxylon* (**RED IRONBARK**); 6025 3rd St./Egbert Ave.

☐ *Sophora japonica* (**JAPANESE PAGODA TREE**); 1751 Newhall St./Revere Ave. The only example of this tree I know of in San Francisco.

BERNAL HEIGHTS

☐ *Eucalyptus camaldulensis* (**RED RIVER GUM**); 144 Cortland Ave./Elsie St. Severely pruned, but a rare tree in San Francisco.

☐ *Eucalyptus nicholii* (**NICHOL'S WILLOW–LEAF PEPPERMINT TREE**); 201–203 Bonview St./Eugenia Ave.

☐ *Eucalyptus sideroxylon* (**RED IRONBARK**); 229 Cortland Ave./Bonview St.; many good examples on Cortland Ave. between Bonview and Mission Sts.

☐ *Fraxinus ornus* (**FLOWERING ASH**); 500 Cortland Ave./Moultrie St., in front of the Bernal Heights Library. One of only a couple of examples of this tree in San Francisco.

☐ *Podocarpus gracilior* (**FERN PINE**); 188 Winfield St./Virginia Ave.

☐ *Acer buergeranum* (**TRIDENT MAPLE**); 6 Ford St./Noe St., in the yard; 3992 20th St./Sanchez St., on Sanchez side, in the planter area.

☐ *Acer saccharinum* (**SILVER MAPLE**); 253 Sanchez St./Market St.

☐ *Aesculus californica* (**CALIFORNIA BUCKEYE**); 124 Lower Terrace.

☐ *Carpinus betulus* (**EUROPEAN HORNBEAM**); 29 Levant St./Roosevelt Way. There are many erect 'Fastigiata' varieties of this tree in the city, but this is the only nonerect example.

☐ *Ceanothus* 'Ray Hartman' (**WILD LILAC**); corner of Sanchez and Liberty Sts.

☐ *Citrus limon* (**LEMON**); 310 Sanchez St./17th St. A rare sidewalk specimen of this tree, which is more often found in backyards.

☐ *Crataegus phaenopyrum* (**WASHINGTON THORN**); 45 Hartford St./17th St. Beautiful when it blooms in June.

☐ *Erythrina crista-galli* (**COCKSPUR CORAL TREE**); 366 Cumberland St./Noe St. This is a spectacular tree, in part because this warmth-loving tree shouldn't be found here. It is one of only a few coral trees in San Francisco.

☐ *Eucalyptus polyanthemos* (**SILVER DOLLAR GUM**); Sanchez St. median near Henry St.

☐ *Jacaranda mimosifolia* (**JACARANDA**); 3970 20th St./Sanchez St.

☐ *Leucadendron argenteum* (**SILVER TREE**); corner of Pemberton and Graystone Terrace. A rare and beautiful tree, and the only example I'm aware of on the city streets.

☐ *Lyonothamnus floribundus* ssp. *asplenifolius* (**CATALINA IRONWOOD**); Hermann St. near corner of Market and Laguna Sts.

☐ *Magnolia grandiflora* (**SOUTHERN MAGNOLIA**); 18th and 20th Sts. between Dolores and Church Sts. (border of Dolores Park).

☐ *Melaleuca quinquenervia* (**CAJEPUT**); 4438–4444 18th St./Douglass St.

☐ *Persea indica* (**MADEIRA BAY**); southwest corner of Dolores Park, near the corner of 20th and Church Sts.

☐ *Phoenix dactylifera* (**DATE PALM**); 1581 Masonic Ave./Upper Terrace.

☐ *Photinia serratifolia* (**CHINESE PHOTINIA**); 4097–4099 19th St./Castro St.

☐ *Pinus torreyana* (**TORREY PINE**); northwest corner of Castro and Henry Sts. (several examples on the hill).

☐ *Platanus orientalis* (**ORIENTAL PLANE TREE**); 3956–3958 19th St./Sanchez St.

☐ *Prunus ilicifolia* (**HOLLYLEAF CHERRY**); 740 Noe St./Liberty St. A California native, but this is the only example I know of on city streets.

☐ *Pseudotsuga menziessi* (**DOUGLAS FIR**); in the side yard at 415 Liberty St./Sanchez St.

☐ *Taxodium distichum* (**BALD CYPRESS**); 486 Roosevelt Way/Lower Terrace. This is a deciduous conifer, shedding its leaves in winter.

☐ *Tristaniopsis laurina* (**SMALL–LEAF TRISTANIA**); 317 Castro St./Market St.

☐ *Ulmus parvifolia* (**CHINESE ELM**); 245–255 Hartford St./19th St.

COLE VALLEY/PARNASSUS HEIGHTS

☐ *Cedrus atlantica* 'Glauca' (**ATLAS CEDAR**); 15 Woodland Ave./Parnassus Ave.

☐ *Ceratonia siliqua* (**CAROB**); 957 Cole St./Parnassus Ave.

☐ *Crataegus laevigata* (**ENGLISH HAWTHORN**); 31 Belmont Ave./Willard St.

☐ *Cryptomeria japonica* (**JAPANESE CRYPTOMERIA**); 185 Edgewood Ave./Belmont Ave.

☐ *Fraxinus ornus* (**FLOWERING ASH**); 110 Edgewood Ave./Farnsworth Lane.

☐ *Malus* (**CRABAPPLE**); 1567 Willard St./Woodland Ave.

☐ *Metrosideros excelsus* (**NEW ZEALAND CHRISTMAS TREE**); rare yellow-flowered 'Aurea' variety at 1221 Stanyan St./17th St. This tree was planted by the late Victor Reiter, a renowned San Francisco horticulturalist.

☐ *Metrosideros robusta* (**NORTHERN RATA**); 893 Clayton St./Parnassus Ave. One of only two known examples in San Francisco outside Golden Gate Park.

☐ *Pinus pinea* (**ITALIAN STONE PINE**); 90 Woodland Ave. (two trees). The house at this address was designed by the famous modernist architect Richard Neutra.

☐ *Pittosporum eugenioides* (**LEMONWOOD**); 575 Belvedere St./Rivoli St.

☐ *Pittosporum undulatum* (**VICTORIAN BOX**); 1403 Willard St./Parnassus Ave.

☐ *Prunus cerasifera* (**PURPLE-LEAF PLUM**); 101 Woodland Ave./Willard St.

☐ *Quercus palustris* (**PIN OAK**); 161 Edgewood Ave./Belmont Ave.

☐ *Quercus suber* (**CORK OAK**); 4736 17th St./Cole St.

☐ *Rhus lancea* (**AFRICAN SUMAC**); 216 Frederick St./Clayton St.

☐ *Ulmus procera* (**ENGLISH ELM**); 78 Woodland Ave./Parnassus Ave.

DOGPATCH

☐ *Acer buergeranum* (**TRIDENT MAPLE**); 704 Tennessee St./18th St.

FINANCIAL DISTRICT

☐ *Alnus cordata* (**ITALIAN ALDER**); corner of Washington St. and the Embarcadero.

☐ *Eucalyptus maculata* (**SPOTTED GUM**); several bordering the Transamerica Pyramid, on Clay St. between Montgomery and Sansome Sts.

☐ *Ginkgo biloba* (**GINKGO**); 804 Montgomery St./Jackson St.; also around the corner at 794 and 798 Jackson St.

☐ *Laurus nobilis* (**SWEET BAY, GRECIAN LAUREL**); 555 Battery St./Jackson St.

☐ *Liriodendron tulipifera* (**TULIP TREE**); northwest corner of Sansome and Sacramento Sts., fronting the old Federal Reserve Bank (many great specimens surround the building).

☐ *Phoenix canariensis* (**CANARY ISLAND PALM**); the Embarcadero at Market St. (many examples).

☐ *Pittosporum crassifolium* (**KARO TREE**); 701 Sansome St./Jackson St.

☐ *Populus nigra* 'Italica' (**LOMBARDY POPLAR**); in the park bordered by the Embarcadero and Washington, Davis, and Clay Sts. (many examples, and these are the trees that San Francisco's wild parrots roost in).

☐ *Sequoia sempervirens* (**COAST REDWOOD**); in the park next to the Transamerica Pyramid.

FOREST HILL

☐ *Araucaria araucana* (**MONKEY PUZZLE TREE**); 2200 9th Ave./Mesa Ave., on the Mesa Ave. side, left of the driveway (female tree). Several Norfolk Island pines (another type of *Araucaria*) are also on this block.

☐ *Cedrus deodara* (**DEODAR CEDAR**); 75 Marcela Ave./Pacheco St. (two trees)

☐ *Fagus sylvatica* (**EUROPEAN BEECH**); 140 Castenada Ave./Magellan Ave.

☐ *Pinus radiata* (**MONTEREY PINE**); 320 Magellan Ave./Dorantes Ave.; 381 Magellan St./Montalvo St. (the Forest Hill Clubhouse at this address was designed by renowned architect Bernard Maybeck).

☐ *Sequoia sempervirens* (**COAST REDWOOD**); across from 185 Castenada Ave./Pacheco St. Sidewalk redwoods are rare, but here is one.

☐ *Taxodium distichum* (**BALD CYPRESS**); 2154 9th Ave./Mendosa Ave.

GLEN PARK

- [ ] *Callistemon viminalis* (**WEEPING BOTTLEBRUSH**); 870 Chenery St./Lippard Ave.
- [ ] *Corymbia ficifolia* (**RED FLOWERING GUM**); across the street from 890 Chenery St./Chilton Ave.
- [ ] *Cupaniopsis anacardioides* (**CARROTWOOD TREE**); 235 Monterey Blvd./Baden St.
- [ ] *Melaleuca nesophila* (**PINK MELALEUCA**); 517 Laidley St./Moffitt St.

HAIGHT-ASHBURY

- [ ] *Alnus cordata* (**ITALIAN ALDER**); in the Golden Gate Park panhandle near the corner of Fell and Shrader Sts.
- [ ] *Juglans nigra* (**BLACK WALNUT**); in the Golden Gate Park panhandle, across from 1809 Oak St./Clayton St.
- [ ] *Koelreuteria paniculata* (**GOLDENRAIN TREE**); 776 Haight St./Scott St.
- [ ] *Laburnum* x *watereri* (**GOLDENCHAIN TREE**); 414 Shrader St./Oak St.
- [ ] *Magnolia campbellii* (**CAMPBELL'S MAGNOLIA**); across from 640 Stanyan St./Page St. in Golden Gate Park.
- [ ] *Maytenus boaria* (**MAYTEN**); in the Golden Gate Park panhandle across from 1685 Oak St./Ashbury St.
- [ ] *Pyrus calleryana* 'Aristocrat' (**CALLERY PEAR**); 436 Cole St./Fell St.
- [ ] *Syncarpia glomulifera* (**TURPENTINE TREE**); across from 63 Scott St., in the park bordering the fence (resembles a New Zealand Christmas tree).

MARINA

- [ ] *Lagerstroemia* 'Natchez' (hybrid of *L. indica* and *L. fauriei*) (**CRAPE MYRTLE**); 60 Rico Way.

MISSION

☐ *Aesculus hippocastanum* (**HORSECHESTNUT**); 945 Dolores St./22nd St.

☐ *Agonis flexuosa* (**PEPPERMINT WILLOW**); 3456 22nd St./Fair Oaks St.

☐ *Albizia julibrissin* (**SILK TREE**); 891 York St./21st St.

☐ *Brachychiton acerifolius* (**FLAME TREE**); 68 Julian St./14th St.; several surrounding the parking lot bounded by Shotwell, 17th, and Folsom Sts. This parking lot is lined with several examples of exotic trees.

☐ *Brachychiton populneus* (**BOTTLE TREE**); several surrounding the parking lot bounded by Shotwell, 17th, and Folsom Sts. (best is near the southwest corner of Folsom and 17th).

☐ *Castanea sativa* (**SPANISH CHESTNUT**); several examples on the south side of 23rd St. between Shotwell and Folsom Sts. (the only examples on San Francisco's streets).

☐ *Chorisia speciosa* 'Majestic Beauty' (**FLOSS SILK TREE**); several surrounding the parking lot bounded by Shotwell, 17th, and Folsom Sts.

☐ *Corymbia citriodora* (**LEMON–SCENTED GUM**); Mission St. just south of Duboce Ave., several trees in the median strip.

☐ *Crinodendron patagua* (**LILY–OF–THE–VALLEY TREE**); 1069–1075 Dolores St./24th St. Only street tree example I know of in San Francisco.

☐ *Eriobotrya japonica* (**LOQUAT**); 905 Florida St./21st St.

☐ *Ficus macrophylla* (**MORETON BAY FIG**); Valencia St. south of Cesar Chavez St., west side of the street near St. Luke's Hospital. This very large specimen is one of San Francisco's best trees.

☐ *Geijera parviflora* (**AUSTRALIAN WILLOW**); 673–675 Guerrero St./22nd St.

☐ *Ginkgo biloba* (**GINKGO**); 1629 Dolores St./29th St.; 3322 22nd St./Valencia St.

☐ *Grevillea robusta* (**SILK OAK**); 3520 18th St./Valencia St.

☐ *Ligustrum lucidum* (**GLOSSY PRIVET**); 1335 Guerrero St./25th St.

☐ *Liquidambar orientalis* (**ORIENTAL SWEETGUM**); across from 547 Dolores St./18th St.; Dolores St. between 20th and 21st Sts., east side of the street.

☐ *Liquidambar styraciflua* (**AMERICAN SWEETGUM**); 2385 Bryant St./22nd St.

☐ *Melaleuca linarifolia* (**FLAXLEAF PAPERBARK**); 170 Albion St./17th St.

☐ *Melaleuca quinquenervia* (**CAJEPUT**); east side of Bryant St. between 18th and Mariposa Sts.

☐ *Melia azedarach* (**CHINABERRY**); 3505 19th St./Valencia St. (the three trees nearest the corner); 1145 Shotwell St./25th st.

☐ *Morus alba* (**WHITE MULBERRY**); 330 Lexington St./20th St.

☐ *Phoenix canariensis* (**CANARY ISLAND PALM**); many examples in the Dolores St. median.

- [ ] *Prunus dulcis* (**ALMOND**); across from 3120 23rd St./Folsom St. (several fruiting trees are interspersed between several Spanish chestnuts).
- [ ] *Prunus cerasifera* (**PURPLE–LEAF PLUM**); 2709 21st St./York St.; 1020–1022 Florida St./22nd St.
- [ ] *Pyrus calleryana* 'Aristocrat' (**CALLERY PEAR**); 2100 block of Bryant St., the tree closest to 20th St.
- [ ] *Quercus lobata* (**VALLEY OAK**); 2830 25th St./Potrero Ave. A California native, but not common in San Francisco.
- [ ] *Robinia* x *ambigua* (**LOCUST**); Bartlett St. on either side of 22nd St. Larger trees south of 22nd St.; smaller trees are the 'Idahoensis' variety.
- [ ] *Sequoiadendron giganteum* (**GIANT SEQUOIA**); Garfield Square, bounded by Harrison St., Treat Ave., 25th and 26th Sts. (several trees).
- [ ] *Taxodium mucronatum* (**MONTEZUMA CYPRESS**); in Dolores Park, directly across from the Christian Science church on Dolores St. between 19th and 20th Sts.
- [ ] *Trachycarpus fortunei* (**WINDMILL PALM**); 17th St. between Florida and Alabama Sts. (both sides).
- [ ] *Washingtonia filifera* (**CALIFORNIA FAN PALM**); Harrison St. between 21st and 22nd Sts., west side of the street (several examples).
- [ ] *Washingtonia robusta* (**MEXICAN FAN PALM**); Mission St. between 15th and 17th Sts. (many examples).

NOB HILL

- [ ] *Dodonaea viscosa* (**HOPSEED**); 1150 Larkin St./Bush St.
- [ ] *Eucalyptus polyanthemos* (**SILVER DOLLAR GUM**); median strip of Van Ness Ave. between O'Farrell and Geary Sts.

NOE VALLEY

- *Acacia dealbata* (**SILVER WATTLE**); 4147 26th St./Noe St. This tree has escaped cultivation in Northern California—you'll see it blooming on Mt. Tamalpais in Marin County in early spring.
- *Acer palmatum* (**JAPANESE MAPLE**); 494 Day St./Castro St.
- *Acer saccharinum* (**SILVER MAPLE**); 499 Eureka St./22nd St.
- *Calocedrus decurrens* (**INCENSE CEDAR**); 514–518 Clipper St./Diamond St.
- *Cinnamomum camphora* (**CAMPHOR**); 3828 Cesar Chavez St./Dolores St.
- *Crataegus phaenopyrum* (**WASHINGTON THORN**); 247 28th St./Church St.
- *Eucalyptus maculata* (**SPOTTED GUM**); downhill from 514–518 Clipper St./ Diamond St.
- *Eucalyptus robusta* (**SWAMP MAHOGANY**); just uphill from 905–907 Diamond St./Jersey St. (three trees). Only examples I know of in San Francisco outside Golden Gate Park.
- *Hymenosporum flavum* (**SWEETSHADE**); 1230–1232 Castro St./24th St.
- *Pittosporum rhombifolium* (**QUEENSLAND PITTOSPORUM**); 1295–1297 Noe St./ 26th St. (second tree from the corner). Only example I know of in San Francisco.
- *Prunus serrulata* (**JAPANESE FLOWERING CHERRY**); 1008–1010 Noe St./23rd St.
- *Quercus agrifolia* (**COAST LIVE OAK**); 1514 Sanchez St./28th St.
- *Rhaphiolepis indica* (**INDIAN HAWTHORN**); 1298 Church St./25th St.
- *Schinus molle* (**CALIFORNIA PEPPER**); 322 28th St./Sanchez St.; 4019 26th St./ Sanchez St.

OMI (OCEANVIEW, MERCED HEIGHTS, INGLESIDE) AND ENVIRONS

- *Acacia baileyana* (**BAILEY'S ACACIA**); 500 Urbano Dr./Borica St.
- *Acacia melanoxylon* (**BLACKWOOD ACACIA**); 1 Northwood Dr./Montecito Ave.
- *Araucaria heterophylla* (**NORFOLK ISLAND PINE**); 98 Lakewood Ave./Fairfield Way near Ocean Ave.
- *Cedrus atlantica* (**ATLAS CEDAR**); 431 Yerba Buena Ave./Monterey Blvd. (two trees).
- *Cupressus macrocarpa* (**MONTEREY CYPRESS**); corner of Cedro Ave. and Mercedes Way.
- *Jubaea chilensis* (**CHILEAN WINE PALM**); 460 Yerba Buena Ave./Monterey Blvd. A beautiful, mature specimen of a slow-growing tree, rare in San Francisco.
- *Leptospurmum laevigatum* (**AUSTRALIAN TEA TREE**); 1249 Alemany Blvd./Silver Ave.; others nearby at 1277 and 1278 Alemany Blvd.

- [ ] *Abies pinsapo* (**SPANISH FIR**); 2522 Octavia St./Vallejo St. A beautiful specimen, and the only example I know of on San Francisco's streets.
- [ ] *Acacia longifolia* (**SYDNEY GOLDEN WATTLE**); across the street from 3931 Sacramento St./Cherry St.
- [ ] *Acer campestre* (**HEDGE MAPLE**); south side of California St. just east of Steiner St. (second tree from the corner). Only example I know of on San Francisco's streets.
- [ ] *Acer macrophyllum* (**BIGLEAF MAPLE**); 2000 block of Franklin St., east side, behind a high retaining wall.
- [ ] *Acer palmatum* (**JAPANESE MAPLE**); 2462–2464 Broadway/Pierce St.
- [ ] *Aesculus carnea* (**RED HORSECHESTNUT**); 2828 Vallejo St./Broderick St. The red candelabra-like flowers of these trees make a great show when they bloom in April.
- [ ] *Alectryon excelsus* (**TITOKI TREE**); 1772 Vallejo St./Gough St. A spectacular specimen of a rare tree—one of my favorite trees in San Francisco.
- [ ] *Alnus rhombifolia* (**WHITE ALDER**); 2050 Buchanan St./California St.
- [ ] *Araucaria bidwillii* (**BUNYA–BUNYA TREE**); 1818 California St./Franklin St. (in the yard, uphill from the house).
- [ ] *Chamaecyparis lawsoniana* (**PORT ORFORD CEDAR**); in Alta Plaza Park, across from 2502–2510 Jackson St.
- [ ] *Erica arborea* (**TREE HEATH**); northeast corner of Alta Plaza Park, corner of Jackson and Steiner Sts.
- [ ] *Eucalyptus globulus* (**BLUE GUM**); 1661 Octavia St./Bush St (several trees). Note the historical sidewalk marker relating to these trees.
- [ ] *Leptospurmum scoparium* (**NEW ZEALAND TEA TREE**); 2065 Vallejo St./Webster St.
- [ ] *Podocarpus gracilior* (**FERN PINE**); 1825 Post St./Fillmore St.
- [ ] *Podocarpus macrophyllus* (**YEW PINE**); directly in front of the Kabuki Theater on Post St. near Fillmore St.
- [ ] *Quercus ilex* (**HOLM OAK, HOLLY OAK**); 1646 Lyon St./Pine St. Only example I know of in San Francisco.
- [ ] *Quercus palustris* (**PIN OAK**); 2155 Filbert St./Webster St.
- [ ] *Quillaja saponaria* (**SOAPBARK TREE**); 2760 Sacramento St./Scott St.; another at 2721 Sacramento St. Beautiful examples of a very rare tree.
- [ ] *Zelkova serrata* (**SAWLEAF ZELKOVA**); 1908 Buchanan St./Bush St. Only example I know of in San Francisco.

POTRERO HILL

- *Acer* x *freemanii* (**FREEMAN MAPLE**); 696 Pennsylvania Ave. (many examples surrounding the building).
- *Callistemon citrinus* (**LEMON BOTTLEBRUSH**); 437–469 Arkansas St./19th St.
- *Carpinus betulus* 'Fastigiata' (**ERECT EUROPEAN HORNBEAM**); 227 Connecticut St./Mariposa St.
- *Lyonothamnus floribundus* ssp. *asplenifolius* (**CATALINA IRONWOOD**); several examples at the northeast corner of 19th St./Connecticut St., adjacent to the church.
- *Melaleuca styphelioides* (**PRICKLY MELALEUCA**); southeast corner of 19th and Missouri Sts. A rare tree in San Francisco.
- *Olea europaea* (**OLIVE**); in the park fronting the 200 block of Carolina St./Mariposa St. (two trees).
- *Persea americana* (**AVOCADO**); 438 Arkansas St./19th St.
- *Pinus patula* (**MEXICAN WEEPING PINE**); 18th St. between Carolina and De Haro Sts., south side of the street.
- *Pyrus kawakamii* (**EVERGREEN PEAR**); 1299 18th St./Texas St.
- *Syagrus romanzoffianum* (**QUEEN PALM**); 1601 Mariposa St./Connecticut St.
- *Washingtonia robusta* (**MEXICAN FAN PALM**); 315 Arkansas St./18th St. This specimen has retained all its fronds.
- *Wigandia urens*; across the street from 1419 18th St./Connecticut St., in the yard, over the fence (the tree with very large purple flowers).

RICHMOND

- *Aesculus californica* (**CALIFORNIA BUCKEYE**); 2694 McAllister St. (at the corner of McAllister St. and Willard St. North). This tree was almost removed due to development in 1999, but the tree-sympathetic property owner changed the development plans, saving the tree.
- *Agonis flexuosa* (**PEPPERMINT WILLOW**); 83–85 Stanyan St./Geary Blvd.
- *Corymbia ficifolia* (**RED FLOWERING GUM**); 608–610 Lake St./7th Ave.
- *Hakea suaveolens* (**SWEET HAKEA**); 1350–1352 Lake St./15th Ave.; 1124–1126 Lake St./12th Ave.
- *Hoheria glabrata* (**MOUNTAIN RIBBONWOOD**); 40 22nd Ave./Lake St.
- *Pittosporum undulatum* (**VICTORIAN BOX**); 132 10th Ave./Lake St.
- *Prunus laurocerasus* (**ENGLISH LAUREL**); 770 3rd Ave./Cabrillo St.
- *Tristania conferta* (**BRISBANE BOX**); 696 2nd Ave./Cabrillo St. A large, stately tree.
- *Umbellularia californica* (**CALIFORNIA BAY**); 2694 McAllister St. (at the corner of McAllister St. and Willard St. North).

RUSSIAN HILL

- ☐ *Acer macrophyllum* (**BIGLEAF MAPLE**); 36 Macondray Lane/Jones St., next to a giant blue gum trunk; also just around the corner in the hillside at the corner of Green and Taylor Sts.
- ☐ *Catalpa speciosa* (**WESTERN CATALPA**); 1154 Chestnut St./Polk St. (in the yard). Only specimen I know of in San Francisco.
- ☐ *Celtis sinensis* (**CHINESE HACKBERRY**); 900 block of Lombard St./Leavenworth St. (many examples).
- ☐ *Pistacia chinensis* (**CHINESE PISTACHE**); 880–884 Lombard St./Jones St.
- ☐ *Pittosporum tenuifolium* (**TARATA PITTOSPORUM**); 1124 Filbert St./Leavenworth St.
- ☐ *Quercus robur* (**ENGLISH OAK**); 819 Francisco St./Hyde St. A rare tree in San Francisco.
- ☐ *Umbellularia californica* (**CALIFORNIA BAY**); just uphill from 1933 Jones St., on Macondray Lane.

ST. FRANCIS WOOD

- ☐ *Cedrus deodara* (**DEODAR CEDAR**); 625 St. Francis Blvd./San Anselmo St.
- ☐ *Corymbia ficifolia* (**RED FLOWERING GUM**); median strip of Monterey Blvd. at the corner of Junipero Serra Blvd.
- ☐ *Fagus sylvatica* (**EUROPEAN BEECH**); 230 Santa Clara Ave./San Anselmo St. (three trees—a beautiful minigrove of beeches).
- ☐ *Pinus radiata* (**MONTEREY PINE**); 214 Santa Clara St./San Anselmo St.
- ☐ *Platanus x acerifolia* (**LONDON PLANE**); the entire length of San Anselmo St. is lined with beautifully pollarded London planes.
- ☐ *Schinus terebinthifolius* (**BRAZILIAN PEPPER**); 350 Santa Ana Ave./Ocean Ave.
- ☐ *Syzygium paniculatum* (**BRUSH CHERRY**); 50 San Buenaventura Way/St. Francis Blvd. (the species lines the entire street, on both sides).

SOUTH OF MARKET (SOMA)

☐ *Alnus rhombifolia* (**WHITE ALDER**); east side of PacBell Park, near Gate 3 to the marina (two rows of trees, in great shape).

☐ *Casuarina stricta* (sometimes referred to as *Casuarina verticullata*) (**MOUNTAIN SHE-OAK**); 407 9th St./Harrison St. (several large, mature trees).

☐ *Eucalyptus sideroxylon* (**RED IRONBARK**); on Folsom St., across from Columbia Alley, near 7th St.

☐ *Ficus microcarpa* (**FICUS**); on Harrison St. between 6th and 7th Sts., south side of the street.

☐ *Fraxinus oxycarpa* 'Raywood' (**RAYWOOD ASH**); many examples on all sides of the building bounded by Harrison, 10th, Bryant, and 11th Sts.

☐ *Platanus x acerifolia* (**LONDON PLANE**); Bryant St. between 6th and 7th Sts., in front of the Hall of Justice.

☐ *Rhamnus alaternus* (**ITALIAN BUCKTHORN**); 1245 Howard St./9th St.

SUNSET

☐ *Arbutus* 'Marina' (**STRAWBERRY TREE**); 1783 10th Ave./Noriega St. (two trees).

☐ *Brachychiton populneus* (**BOTTLE TREE**); 536 Judah St./11th Ave. More common in Southern California, this tree braves the chilly Sunset neighborhood.

☐ *Chiranthodendron pentadactylon* (**MONKEY HAND TREE**); 954 Irving St./11th Ave. (on 11th Ave. side). Only example I know of on San Francisco's streets.

☐ *Cordyline australis* (**GIANT DRACAENA**); across from 1963 9th Ave./Pacheco St.

☐ *Corynocarpus laevigata* (**NEW ZEALAND LAUREL**); 1220 9th Ave./Lincoln Way. Only street tree example I know of in San Francisco.

☐ *Eriobotrya deflexa* (**BRONZE LOQUAT**); 1241 7th Ave./Lincoln Way

☐ *Ilex aquifolium* (**ENGLISH HOLLY**); 1665 8th Ave./Moraga St. A spectacular specimen of this tree.

☐ *Michelia doltsopa* (**MICHELIA**); 326 Kirkham St./7th Ave.

☐ *Tilia cordata* (**LITTLE-LEAF LINDEN**); 1955 9th Ave./Pacheco St.

TELEGRAPH HILL/NORTH BEACH

☐ *Cinnamomum camphora* (**CAMPHOR**); 418 Union St./Kearny St.

☐ *Lagunaria patersonii* (**PRIMROSE TREE, COW ITCH TREE**); across from 1660 Stockton St./Filbert St. in the corner of Washington Square Park (three large specimens).

☐ *Maytenus boaria* (**MAYTEN**); near the corner of Columbus Ave. and Union St., in Washington Square Park.

☐ *Melaleuca linarifolia* (**FLAXLEAF PAPERBARK**); 461 Chestnut St./Powell St.

☐ *Podocarpus gracilior* (**FERN PINE**); 752 Vallejo St./Emery St.

☐ *Salix matsudana* 'Tortuosa' (**TWISTED HANKOW WILLOW**); across from 629 Union St./Columbus Ave. in Washington Square Park.

TENDERLOIN

☐ *Araucaria heterophylla* (**NORFOLK ISLAND PINE**); 606 Ellis St./Hyde St. Unusual to find this large a tree in this dense an urban environment.

WEST PORTAL

☐ *Araucaria bidwillii* (**BUNYA–BUNYA TREE**); 201 Vicente St./Wawona St. One of San Francisco's best trees, and very near another exotic *Araucaria*—a monkey puzzle tree *(Araucaria araucana)* at 290 Wawona St.

☐ x *Chiranthofremontia lenzii*; 858 Portola Dr./Laguna Honda Blvd.—a rare hybrid of two genera: *Chiranthodendron* and *Fremontodendron* 'Pacific Sunset'.

WESTERN ADDITION/NORTH OF PANHANDLE

☐ *Acacia melanoxylon* (**BLACKWOOD ACACIA**); 740 Masonic Ave./Hayes St.

☐ *Acer rubrum* (**RED MAPLE**); 345 Grove St./Franklin St.

☐ *Eucalyptus globulus* (**BLUE GUM**); 1100 block of Laguna St./Turk St. in Jefferson Square Park.

☐ *Fraxinus uhdei* (**EVERGREEN ASH; SHAMEL ASH**); 501 Masonic Ave./McAllister St.

☐ *Pinus canariensis* (**CANARY ISLAND PINE**); median strip of Geary St., either side of Laguna St.

☐ *Populus alba* (**WHITE POPLAR**); corner of Ellis and Steiner Sts., in Raymond Kimball playground.

☐ *Quillaja saponaria* (**SOAPBARK TREE**); 736–738 Masonic Ave./Hayes St. Rare in San Francisco.

☐ *Salix babylonica* (**WEEPING WILLOW**); across from 1104 Fulton St./Pierce St. in Alamo Square Park.

The Artist Rigo

ONE TREE

One Tree is one of the best-known works by Rigo 03, a San Francisco artist whose monumental outdoor paintings often mimic familiar signage. One Tree is painted on a wall next to the on-ramp to Highway 101 at the corner of Bryant and 10th Sts. in the SOMA (South of Market) neighborhood. Like many of his works, this piece uses a tongue-in-cheek twist on familiar icons to deliver a message. In this mural, Rigo had some fun with the familiar one-way sign, which, in addition to its traffic connotation, also had undesirable authoritarian associations for the artist.

According to Rigo, the location of One Tree came before any inspiration for the art. In planning the piece, Rigo first fretted over how to work around the tree to the right of the wall. But then he realized that his notion of the tree being an obstacle to the art was exactly backward! In that epiphany, Rigo realized that One Tree was the perfect theme for the wall. Instead of promoting "one way," trees were a form of life that branched out in many directions, both aboveground and below.

Where else can you find works by Rigo? They are always at risk of disappearing as billboards or buildings go up, but here are few: Extinct (behind the Shell station at the corner of 5th and Folsom Sts.); Innercity/Home (on 6th St. between Folsom and Howard Sts.); Birds/Cars at 1712 Bryant St./16th St.; and Truth (at the corner of Market and 7th Sts.). Born Ricardo Gouveia on Madeira Island, Rigo came to the Bay Area to study art, receiving degrees from the San Francisco Art Institute and Stanford University. By the time you read this, Rigo will likely be Rigo 04—since in January of every year he has his legal name changed to reflect the current year. Why? "It's my way of inoculating myself with a little of the poison from the inundation of numbers we face, and reclaiming it as my own," Rigo has said. And what about the tree? It's a silver dollar eucalyptus *(Eucalyptus polyanthemos)*.

SELECTED BIBLIOGRAPHY

Boland, D., M. Brooker, G. Chippendale, N. Hall, B. Hyland, R. Johnston, D. Kleinig, and J. Turner. *Forest Trees of Australia*, 4th ed. Collingwood, Victoria, Australia: CSIRO Publishing, 1999.

Brenzel, Kathleen N., ed. *Western Garden Book*. Menlo Park, CA: Sunset Publishing, 2001.

Donat, Hank. *MisterSF.com*. Website: www.mistersf.com.

Friends of the Urban Forest. *Trees for San Francisco*, 2nd ed., 1995.

Hodel, Donald R. *Exceptional Trees of Los Angeles*. Los Angeles: California Arboretum Foundation, 1988.

Jacobson, Arthur Lee. *Trees of Seattle*. Seattle: Sasquatch Books, 1989.

Johnson, Hugh. *The International Book of Trees*. New York: Simon & Schuster, 1973.

L. H. Bailey Hortorium staff. *Hortus Third: A Concise Dictionary of Plants Cultivated in the United States and Canada*. New York: Macmillan Publishing Company, 1976.

McClintock, Elizabeth; Richard G. Turner, Jr., ed. *The Trees of Golden Gate Park*. Berkeley, CA: Heyday Books/Clapperstick Institute, 2001.

Metcalf, Woodbridge. *Introduced Trees of Central California*. Berkeley and Los Angeles: University of California Press, 1968.

Muller, Katherine K., Richard E. Broder, and Will Beittel. *Trees of Santa Barbara*. Santa Barbara, CA: Santa Barbara Botanic Garden, 1974.

Plotnik, Arthur. *The Urban Tree Book*. New York: Three Rivers Press, 2000.

Reynolds, Phyllis C. and Elizabeth F. Dimon. *Trees of Greater Portland*. Portland: Timber Press, 1993.

Straley, Gerald B. *Trees of Vancouver*. Vancouver: UBC Press, 1992.

cluster pine
Pinus pinaster, 128
coast live oak
Quercus agrifolia, 139
coast redwood
Sequoia sempervirens, 93, 94, 108, 115, 135
cockspur coral tree
Erythrina crista-galli, 38, 133
cork oak
Quercus suber, 89, 111, 134
cow itch tree, primrose tree
Lagunaria patersonii, 85, 144
crabapple
Malus, 134
crape myrtle
Lagerstoemia 'Natchez', 136

D

date palm
Phoenix dactylifera, 133
deodar cedar
Cedrus deodara, 25, 109, 128, 135, 142
Douglas fir
Pseudotsuga menziessi, 79, 133
drooping melaleuca
Melaleuca armillaris, 85

E

empress tree
Paulownia tomentosa, 105
English elm
Ulmus procera, 107, 134
English hawthorn
Crataegus laevigata, 31, 32, 34, 134
English holly
Ilex aquifolium, 143
English laurel
Prunus laurocerasus, 141
English oak
Quercus robur, 142
European beech
Fagus sylvatica, 135, 142
European hornbeam
Carpinus betulus, 123, 133, 141
evergreen ash, shamel ash
Fraxinus uhdei, 45, 144
evergreen pear
Pyrus kawakamii, 84, 88, 116, 123, 141

F

fern pine
Podocarpus gracilior, 132, 141, 144
ficus, Indian laurel fig
Ficus microcarpa, 44, 84, 120, 123, 128, 143
flame tree
Brachychiton acerifolius, 121, 137
flaxleaf paperbark
Melaleuca linarifolia, 67, 85, 119, 137, 144
floss silk tree
Chorisia speciosa 'Majestic Beauty', 121, 137
flowering ash
Fraxinus ornus, 108, 132, 134
flowering plum
Prunus x *blireiana,* 85
Freeman maple
Acer x *freemanii,* 141

G

giant dracaena, cabbage palm
Cordyline australis, 28, 68, 108, 143
giant sequoia
Sequoiadendron giganteum, 94, 138
ginkgo, maidenhair
Ginkgo biloba, 47–48, 84, 108, 111, 112, 116, 121, 135, 137
glossy privet
Ligustrum lucidum, 58, 84, 124, 137
golden chain tree
Laburnum x *watereri,* 136
golden rain tree
Koelreuteria paniculata, 112, 136
Grecian laurel, sweet bay
Laurus nobilis, 27, 54, 103, 108, 117, 127, 135

H

hedge maple
Acer campestre, 140
hollyleaf cherry
Prunus ilicifolia, 111, 133
holm oak, holly oak
Quercus ilex, 140
hopseed
Dodonaea viscosa, 36, 84, 138
horsechestnut
Aesculus hippocastanum, 137

INDEX OF TREES
BY SCIENTIFIC NAME